"License to Sell really paints the whole picture of selling. Too often, we think selling is waiting for the phone to ring and then placing the business where you're told. That's not selling, it's facilitating an inquiry. This book will guide you through the difference and identify, enhance, and highlight your skills."

Bruce J. Himelstein, Senior Vice President,
Field Sales North America, Marriott International

"One of those rare finds that teaches you the tools you need to seal the deal."

Kristin L. Penta, Creator of Fun Cosmetics

"This is a must read for any front line sales rep through senior sales executive! Everyone will gain a new technique from prospecting to relationship building to negotiation. In simple terms License to Sell is a rich collection of common sense approaches to sales and negotiation. However, it goes much further by: including techniques for today's business environment, showing effective ways of incorporating electronic means of communication into your process, and expanding the way you view the sales process."

Paul H. Brown, III
SkillSoft "Learning on Demand" Corporation

"This book will guarantee you'll always be one step ahead of the competition."

Ann Marie Wilson, Owner, Pretty Woman and Suits You Consignment Shops

"Your relationship is the unique difference you can create with your customers - particularly when products and services are more alike than ever before. License to Sell provides an outstanding road map to building relationships."

David C. Miles, Chairman, The Miles/LeHane Group

"A must read! This excellent guide gives practical tips and step by step tools to enhance sales capability. A mandatory resource for all sales training classes."

Marcie Mueller, Manager, Training SatoTravel

"As global providers of complex logistics solutions, with clients and associates in every time-zone around the world, face-to-face selling is quickly becoming the exception. Electronic and telephone selling must be compressed and highly responsive to be effective. License to Sell is a valuable, plain-speaking guide that arms the reader with tools and techniques that you can use to close deals across the conference table or several continents."

Phil Genovese, Director Contract Logistics, Fritz Companies, Inc.

"*License to Sell* is a weapon every professional salesperson should have in his arsenal."
>Tom Delehanty, GlobeCast Communications/Professional Actor

"The long term key to success in selling, regardless of the business, is to build strong, mutually beneficial relationships with customers. As our world transitions from an "information" to "knowledge" society, we will need new tools to succeed in a vastly transformed marketplace. License to Sell provides an excellent road map and strategic approach to making this happen."
>Ed Nielsen, President & CEO, International Association of Convention & Visitor Bureaus (IACVB)

"Great trends! Great techniques! Great book!"
>Carmel King, VP/COO, The IMAS Publishing Group

"I make a lot of in-home sales calls. The book paid for itself on the first call. It's money in your pocket."
>Mark Elia, President Mark of Excellence Remodeling, Inc.

"The book is simple, user friendly, and the best book on sales training I've ever seen!"
>Roy B. Evans, Jr., CAE, President & CEO, Professional Convention Management Association (PCMA)

"Practical and easy to read . . . follow these veteran sales executive's methods and advice to successful selling."
>Pam Farr, President, The Cabot Group

"This valuable text proves that selling is not art but science. Mr. Ilvento and Mr. Price demonstrate page after page methods that unlock the secrets of sales success. This book is now required reading for all of my sales and marketing associates."
>Philip M. Warner, Director of Marketing, U-Metco Inc.

"Very practical and relevant. Skills that you can apply immediately."
>Marilyn and Denyse, The Madison Consulting Company

"Joe and Doug bring real-life experiences that make this a must-read book for anyone serious about a career in sales."
>Mike Gamble, Senior Vice President Sales & Marketing, Philadelphia Convention & Visitors Bureau

"I've been a sales rep for for 20 years and to those who say you can't teach an old dog new tricks — Woof!"
>Michael Zelich, Michael Zelich Associates, Inc.

LICENSE TO SELL

Also by Joseph C. Ilvento

BOOKS

Nobody to Somebody in 63 Days or Less

MONOGRAPH

Selling Strategies for Changing Economic Times

Joe Ilvento

Doug Price

LICENSE TO SELL

Professional Field Guide to Selling Skills & Market Trends

Applied Business Communications, Inc.
New Jersey

Acknowledgment

We would like to thank Tracy Ilvento, who invested her editorial, design and publishing skills into this book. Without her interest and support, this book would still be in bits and pieces on our brains and hard drives.

He and she have been used interchangeably throughout this book to represent both men and women who have chosen sales as their profession.

Copyright © 1999, Applied Business Communications, Inc.

All rights reserved. No part of this book may be used or reproduced in any manner whatsoever without the written permission of the Publisher.

Printed in the United States of America.

ABC, Inc. 29 Maple, Suite 100, West Long Branch, New Jersey 07764

ISBN 0-9654362-2-5

To our fathers, who understood the importance of selling and the art of building relationships.

Joe Ilvento

If Joe Ilvento is not a born salesman, he became one early in life. As a kid selling greeting cards door-to-door, he learned the concept of prospecting, rejection and the fact that sales is a numbers game that requires persistence and skill. Joe soon learned that as his selling skills increased, the number of doors he had to knock on to make a sale became less and less. This business lesson was learned at age 10. His first corporate sales position after getting his psychology degree from Syracuse University was with Cable & Wireless Communications. Within a couple of months he rose up the ranks to become their top salesperson, exceeding the company's quota of 20 new customers per month by as many as 130 and breaking the old record of 57. They said, in short, "Joe you know how to sell this stuff – now we want you to teach everyone in the company how you do it." At the ripe old age of 23, he was promoted to a national sales trainer position for the company and was responsible for teaching all new sales representatives how to sell.

His sales talents did not go unrecognized. He then joined Learning International (formally Xerox Learning Systems) as a Professional Selling Skills sales training consultant and ultimately rose to the position of one of only 13 Master Trainers worldwide.

Over the last 10 years, he has acted as President of a sales and marketing consulting firm dedicated to helping others with their sales and marketing requirements. He has worked closely and held long-term consulting contracts with such firms as Citibank, Guerrilla Marketing International and Fred Pryor Seminars. Joe has personally trained over 15,000 business people around the world in such places as Australia, the United Kingdom and every major city in the United States.

Past audience members have included numerous government agencies such as the Central Intelligence Agency, the Marines, the Air Force, the Treasury Department, the Secret Service, and Army National Guard. Private sector audience members have included Citibank, MCI/WorldCom, Printing Industries of America, the National Real Estate Institute of America, Marriott, First Union Bank, Royal Insurance, Bechtel, the Family Research Council, Ford Motors, and more.

Joe's first book *Nobody to Somebody in 63 Days or Less* (available at Amazon.com) shows people how to use word of mouth advertising and referral selling to dramatically increase sales. He has appeared in newspapers, magazines and on various radio and television shows including the *Bloomburg Financial Network*, *WPGC Business News Radio*, *Entrepreneur's Radio Showcase*, and the *Business as Unusual* television show.

Joe Ilvento specializes in developing the selling skills of others. He delivers, one-day, sales and marketing workshops designed for novice or seasoned sales professionals. His seminars are interactive, applied, fun, and most of all effective. Joe can be reached at 1-800-382-6343 or by e-mail at joeilvento@home.com.

Doug Price, CMP

Doug Price is an authority on sales and marketing. For more than 25 years, he has sold everything from Fuller Brushes to meetings and conventions to Executive Coaching. Doug's approach to selling was shaped with direct sales jobs as a teenager and in large-part by 18 years of selling conventions for Marriott Hotels, Resorts, and Suites. His passion for sales earned him numerous sales incentive awards and Doug was named Marriott's Rookie Director of Marketing of the Year in 1983. He also served as Marriott's Vice President of Employment Marketing and Director of Sales Training and Development. In 1995, he started Keystone Consulting with a focus on designing and delivering interactive sales training for clients.

Doug feels that his philosophy towards sales was shaped very early in life. His father, Harry Price, was a salesman his whole life, primarily selling ranges and kitchen appliances for Caloric and Tappan. As a child, Doug was introduced to many of his dad's clients throughout his sales territory in Ohio. Doug enjoyed riding in the car with his dad on sales calls. His dad mixed business and pleasure very well. Often the Price family entertained customers in their home and vice versa. Those early lessons on building relationships stayed with him.

Like many successful salespeople, Doug started early in sales with a newspaper route delivering a "free weekly paper." As a carrier, the only way to make money was to try and collect the "suggested donation" of 50 cents per month. The only reason people would pay for a free weekly paper was if the carrier placed the paper exactly where the customer wanted it each Wednesday morning. The carrier also had to be persistent in following up to catch people when they might be home to pay. Doug learned customer service and timely follow-up delivering "free papers" and consistently winning sales contests among carriers.

Selling Fuller Brushes at the age of 15 taught Doug how to handle rejection and use testimonials. As he would work door-to-door getting rejected, he realized that sales is a numbers game. Not everybody was going to buy and you couldn't take a "NO" answer personally. Instead, he learned to be happy that he didn't waste time giving a sales pitch to an uninterested buyer. Once Doug made a sale, he would tell the next person he called on what their neighbor up the street had purchased. When the neighbor heard what someone else had decided to buy, selling became easier. Testimonials are still very powerful today in selling.

Selling Marriott Hotels, Resorts, and Suites for eighteen years crystallized the importance of building and maintaining relationships with customers. In the highly competitive world of hotel sales, properties compete to convince meeting planners, along with business and leisure travelers to stay at their facility. Anyone who travels knows there are hotels everywhere and the choices range from no frills to full frills. Doug found that getting to know his customers as well as their needs was a key element in separating him from his competition. Customers buy the salespeople as well as their products/services — and the better you know a customer — the more likely you make a sale. Doug has actually had the honor of delivering a eulogy at a customer's funeral. That represented a true relationship!

Today, Doug Price is President of The Miles/LeHane Group in Leesburg, Virginia. The company designs and delivers sales training and career management consulting with a focus on executive development in the areas of Outplacement, Career Coaching, and Executive Search. Recent appearances by Doug include *Tomorrow's Business* on CNN Business Radio and CBS *Eye on Business*.

If you need services that are customized and interactive, contact Doug Price at 703-777-3370 or by e-mail at feedback@mileslehane.com.

CONTENTS

Foreword by Roger Dow   xv

Sales Trends

BECOMING A CUSTOMER CHAMPION
Customers Want It Now	21
Convenience, Inventory & Price	25
Sound Bite Presentations	29

THE 21st CENTURY SALESPERSON
Customized Presentations that Sell Don't Tell	35
Expertise is Mandatory and Expected	39
Applied Competency	43
Perceptions of Trust & Credibility	47
The Salesperson as Orchestrator	51

SALES-EDGE TECHNOLOGY
Real-Time Selling	57
Remote Interaction with Customers	61
Virtual Storefronts	65

BETTER, FASTER, DIFFERENT SELLING STRATEGIES
Easy Access Business Profile	71
Virtual Companies	75
Branding and Electronic Cash	79
Upgrades and Enhancements	83
Partner with a Complementary Company or Competitor	87
Defect Reduction	91
Selling Quality	95

LICENSE TO SELL

Sales Skills

BEFORE THE SALE

Prospecting 101 and Beyond	*99*
Prospecting for New Customers	*103*
The Art of Asking Questions	*107*
Qualifying — It's All in the Questions	*111*
Outbound Telemarketing is Proactive	*115*
Gatekeepers & Voice Mail	*117*
The Sales Cycle	*125*

DURING THE SALE

Relationship Building: You are the Initial Product	*129*
Customer Traits	*133*
Benefit Selling: Transitioning from Features to Tactical Benefits	*137*
Adding Value to What You Sell	*143*
Selling Against the Competition	*145*
Buying Signals	*151*
Psychology & Traits of the Super Salesperson	*155*
The Art of Closing	*159*

AFTER THE SALE

How to Turn Objections into Opportunities	*177*
Negotiation Skills	*183*
Put Yourself Next in Line	*195*
Follow-Up — You'll Be Hearing from Me	*197*

Foreword
by
Roger Dow

You are about to read a book that will help both the first-time salesperson and the seasoned pro with their ability to sell in today's business world and the electronic one that will be upon us faster than you can spell *e-commerce*. Traditional face-to-face selling relationships will always be critical, however, to survive in the future, one must also capitalize on the trends that are transforming the way we do business. The Internet, telephone, interactive TV, cell phones, and computers are all modern day tools salespeople must incorporate into their overall strategies for success. This book provides a glimpse into the future of selling and will equip you with the professional selling skills needed to *make the sale* and remain competitive.

License to Sell is really two books in one. The first part focuses on 18 *Sales Trends* that will dramatically impact the way you do business now and, more importantly, in the future. The second part provides you with both basic and advanced Sales Skills for 2000 and Beyond which every professional salesperson must own and master to be relevant and valued by their organization and the customers.

What makes this book truly a "hands on — real world" development tool are the *Missions*. These missions are interactive exercises designed to get you thinking and applying what you learn page after page, chapter after chapter. I hope you don't skim over the missions — take the time to pause and think about the questions Joe and Doug pose to you. Make the investment in yourself and complete each of the missions you are assigned. Speaking from experience, they will get you thinking and acting strategically and provide you with the competitive insights necessary to out-sell your competition.

Foreword

Also, I found the *Top Secret* tips to be valuable insights. These secret messages are quick, to-the-point learnings pulled from the reading. They underscore the key learning themes and will stimulate your strategic thinking.

As an executive for Marriott for the last 25 years and the co-author of *Turned On*, I have been involved with the art of selling for most of my life. Each year, I speak to thousands of business people and one core theme that hopefully comes through in each presentation I make is the concept that *selling is everything!* Whether you are selling ideas, products, or services. Whether you are selling to internal customers like your boss or other department heads or external customers like your customers and prospects – your *ability to influence others* is the biggest single factor in determining your success in life. Knowing what to say, what questions to ask, what questions not to ask, and how to handle customer attitudes is as much an art as it is a skill. *License to Sell* will provide you with the knowledge of how to master the skills of influence. More importantly, the book will provide you with the insights on how the application of these skills will change as we move towards doing business electronically.

Think of *License to Sell* as a full-blown Master's course that has knowledge, workbooks, selected readings, and written exercises all wrapped into a 200-page book. As the title implies, in a very short period of time, the salesperson of yesterday will risk becoming a dinosaur when compared to the salesperson of tomorrow. Salespeople of tomorrow must earn their *License to Sell* to the customers of tomorrow. These customers will demand more expertise, more product knowledge, faster turn-around, more flexibility, and more product and service customization than ever before.

It will only be those salespeople who are *Licensed to Sell* – those who understand the demands of evolving new customers and possess the selling skills necessary to meet and exceed their needs – that will succeed. Once you have read the book and completed all the mission exercises, you will have earned your *License to Sell*.

Foreword

This License will provide you with the competitive edge necessary to travel far beyond today's physical sales territories and geographic boundaries. A *License to Sell* is your passport to sell and service customers in an exciting global marketplace that operates (7 x 24 x 365) 24 hours a day, seven days a week, 365 days a year. I wish you success in your sales journey into the future.

Roger Dow

Roger Dow is Senior Vice President/General Sales Manager for Marriott International and co-author of *Turned On — Eight Vital Insights to Energize Your People, Customers, and Profits.*

BECOMING A CUSTOMER CHAMPION

Customers Want It Now

★

Convenience, Inventory & Price

★

Sound Bite Presentations

LICENSE TO SELL

Customers Want It Now

One trend that is transforming the expectations associated with the delivery of products and services to the customer is directly related to the question, *when can I get it?* If your answer is now, you're a giant step closer to earning the customer's business.

Today, overnight mail, e-mail, microwave ovens, computer software, high speed copy machines, and yes, even pizza delivery has changed the customer's expectations of *when can I get it?* Every industry is unique, but if a competitor is able to service your customer faster, better or less expensively, a precedent has been set. The bar has risen, and it is only a matter of time before the customer will demand the same level of service from you and your company.

The world economy is here and with it customer expectations are rising faster than ever before. As a professional salesperson you must take personal responsibility to do what it takes to meet, and whenever possible, exceed your customers' needs for timely delivery of products and services. Failure to do so leaves the door wide open for a competitor who can do it faster than you can.

TOP SECRET

If a competitor is able to get to your customer faster, better or less expensively than you can, a precedent has been set. It is only a matter of time before the customer will demand the same level of service from you.

LICENSE TO SELL

YOUR MISSION

The salesperson who can provide customers with *what* they want, *when* they want it — wins. Your mission is to use the following questions as part of your intelligence gathering to capitalize on the *Customers Want It Now* trend.

❏ Document the delivery process of your product or service. Set improvement goals. How long does it take you now to deliver on a customer need? How long does it take your biggest competitor?

_____
_____
_____
_____

❏ Does your product or service traditionally require the customer to come to you? If so, is there a way you can bring it to your customer?

_____
_____
_____
_____

❏ If you tend to custom order what customers require, is there a way to keep a small inventory of the most requested items on hand?

_____
_____
_____
_____

Becoming a Customer Champion

❑ How can you use the Internet or e-mail to speed the way you do business in terms of getting documents, brochures and catalogs in the hands of your customers?

_____
_____
_____
_____
_____

❑ How could the purchase of new equipment, hardware or software speed the way you do business with your customers?

_____
_____
_____
_____
_____

❑ If you can't change your industry, product or service, what can you as a salesperson personally do to better meet or exceed your customers' expectations?

_____
_____
_____
_____
_____

LICENSE TO SELL

Convenience, Inventory & Price

The choice that salespeople of the past used to give their customers was *take it or leave it*. The trend now and into the future is total customer customization. Surveys show that customers prefer megastores and franchises — even catalogs, TV and on-line Internet shopping — over the traditional limited inventory, locally owned retail shops with only a few exceptions. Why? People prefer convenience, inventory and price. Extended hours, quick access to huge inventories, and the best price are strong influencers when it comes to deciding how and where to purchase a product or service.

Interestingly, there are a few exceptions that can work to the local retailer's advantage when trying to compete against convenience, inventory and price. They are *personalized service* and the fact that people prefer to deal with *experts* and will pay a premium to do so.

> **TOP SECRET**
> *Smaller local vendors can compete against convenience, inventory and price by capitalizing on personalized service and expertise.*

LICENSE TO SELL

YOUR MISSION

Your mission is to use the following questions as part of your intelligence gathering to capitalize on the *Convenience, Inventory & Price* trend.

❏ How quickly are you able to service your customers?

_____
_____
_____
_____

❏ From the moment of first contact to the moment a customer has the product or service in hand, how long does it take?

_____
_____
_____
_____

❏ What can you do to more quickly meet your customer needs?

_____
_____
_____
_____
_____
_____
_____

Becoming a Customer Champion

❏ What inventory can you stock? What products can you offer in the form of a virtual inventory?

_____
_____
_____
_____

❏ How are your products priced compared to your competitors? What can you do to add value to each and every sale?

_____
_____
_____
_____

❏ What can you do to differentiate yourself from your competition?

_____
_____
_____
_____

❏ What new level of service can you provide to your customers?

_____
_____
_____
_____

27

LICENSE TO SELL

Sound Bite Presentations

Year 2000 and beyond customers are often referred to as the TV generation. Why? In part because many have been raised from childhood with a TV remote control in their hands. They are accustomed to — and expect — presentations that mirror TV commercials which are short, effective and have a purpose. When they don't like something — click — and they're off to a new channel.

Yesterday it was the click of a TV remote. Today it is the click of a mouse. Good salespeople must be able to capture and hold the attention of the year 2000 and beyond customer. The days of customers playing the role of polite listeners are gone, and short, concise sales presentations are in.

> **TOP SECRET**
>
> *Real-time access to knowledge, product information, competitor information, financing options, delivery schedules, etc., must be a click away.*

LICENSE TO SELL

YOUR MISSION

Your mission is to use the following questions as part of your intelligence gathering to capitalize on the *Sound Bite Presentations* trend.

❑ What one statement or question could you state that would capture a customer's attention?

_____
_____
_____
_____
_____
_____
_____

❑ What are three needs/problems your customers have that your product can solve?

1. _____
_____
2. _____
_____
3. _____
_____
_____

Becoming a Customer Champion

❏ If you had to sell your product or service in 60 seconds or less what would you say?

_____
_____
_____
_____
_____
_____
_____
_____
_____

❏ If you had to convince a customer to use your product over a competitor's in 30 seconds or less, what would you say?

_____
_____
_____
_____
_____
_____
_____
_____
_____

LICENSE TO SELL

THE 21ST CENTURY SALESPERSON

Customized Presentations that Sell Don't Tell

★

Expertise is Mandatory and Expected

★

Applied Competency

★

Perceptions of Trust & Credibility

★

The Salesperson As Orchestrator

LICENSE TO SELL

The 21st Century Salesperson

Customized Presentations that Sell Don't Tell

Today's salesperson has to confront a more educated consumer who has more purchase options available than ever before. Consequently, the successful salesperson must be able to meet the needs of the customer quickly, effectively and do so in a friendly manner. The days of long, drawn-out presentations are gone along with the razzle-dazzle of a canned script. Not to say that this old-style selling approach will not work, it may still work on some, but don't underestimate the year 2000 and beyond customer. To succeed, you must genuinely know how to sell — not tell.

21st century salespeople must customize their presentations by answering the question in the customer's mind, *what's in it for me?* Today's customers don't have time to educate the salesperson, so making a sales presentation that is the equivalent of covering all the features and benefits of your products and services just won't cut it anymore. Skilled year 2000 and beyond salespeople will use *strategic probing*, along with doing their *homework* before interacting with customers.

Successful salespeople will be consultative. They ask questions and never assume that what they have to sell will satisfy the customer's need 100%, at least in the beginning. Often, the sale will be made when the customer realizes that it may cost more to do *nothing* about their current situation than to do something about it. It is the job of the salesperson to show the customer how he will save money (or make money) with the use of the product or service. One must present a value-laden presentation customized to the exact needs of the prospect.

TOP SECRET

The year 2000 and beyond sale will emphasize different selling features: consumer-based custom presentations. The salesperson must be an expert.

LICENSE TO SELL

YOUR MISSION

Your mission is to use the following questions as part of your intelligence gathering to capitalize on the *Customized Presentations that Sell Don't Tell* trend. One of your jobs as a consultative salesperson is to illustrate to the customer *what the cost is for continuing with the status quo.*

Complete the 10 open-ended questions below that you might use to be consultative.

1. Who..
2. What...
3. Why...
4. When...
5. Where...
6. Tell me...
7. Explain...
8. Describe...
9. How...
10. Demonstrate...

❏ How long is your average presentation?

❏ What percentage of time is used for consultative questions and determining customer needs?

❏ How much does the current customer problem cost the customer in terms of money, time, effort, and lost opportunity, on a per instance basis?

Daily: _____

Weekly: _____

Monthly: _____

Annually: _____

❏ How important is the problem to the customer?

_____

_____

❏ How often is the problem occurring?

_____

_____

❏ How many customers have been lost due to the problem? Annually?

_____

_____

❏ If applicable, how many days/years would it take for the savings associated with your product or service to pay for itself? To start making a profit for the customer?

_____

_____

❏ What is the value of a customer (profit) per year/sale? What is the lifetime value of a customer?

_____

_____

LICENSE TO SELL

Expertise is Mandatory and Expected

The salesperson entering the 21st century must be an expert in his or her field. Today, smart customers expect direct answers to direct questions. Customers making a major purchase will almost always obtain two or three price quotes or proposals prior to making a decision. This multiple quote approach often turns the customer into a quasi-expert. Comparing one salesperson's presentation to another's creates challenging and insightful questions.

Bottom line: There should be no doubt in the customer's mind that you possess expert product knowledge. If there is any doubt or hesitation present on the part of the salesperson, it will translate into hesitation to do business with you. With price being equal, the more competent salesperson will almost always prevail. If your price is higher than that of your competition, your expertise must be sold and perceived by the customer as an added value of doing business with you. If you are the expert and your price is lowest, there will be no stopping you.

> **TOP SECRET**
>
> *Customers today and into the future expect straight answers to straight questions. Bottom line: there should be no doubt in the customer's mind that you possess expert product knowledge.*

LICENSE TO SELL

YOUR MISSION

Your mission is to prioritize your expertise and knowledge curve as part of your intelligence gathering to capitalize on the *Expertise is Mandatory and Expected* trend.

❏ Write down the 10 most common questions that customers ask about your business or industry.

_____
_____
_____
_____
_____
_____
_____
_____
_____
_____

❏ Write down the 10 most common questions that customers ask about your product or service.

_____
_____
_____
_____
_____
_____
_____

❏ Write down the 10 most common questions that customers might ask to compare your product or service with that of your competitors.

❏ Now, within each section, rank the questions in the order that customers would most likely ask them. Take the time to develop clear, concise answers using objective evidence (newspaper and magazine articles, testimonials, pictures, demonstrations, free samples/trials) to support your answers.

LICENSE TO SELL

The 21st Century Salesperson

Applied Competency

Technology is racing to replace the human face-to-face interaction in today's business environment. Why? There is competency in technology. For example, why do you prefer to do your banking with an ATM as opposed to a teller? The ATM works on your schedule 24 hours a day, seven days a week, 365 days a year — unlike a teller. The ATM does what you want it to do — no more and no less. And, the ATM doesn't have an attitude. Now that may sound cynical, but in today's business world, competency is key. A smart machine does exactly what it is told to do quickly and efficiently.

You must become your customer's ATM — regardless of the products or services you sell. Ideally, the customer comes to you and initiates the transaction. If that is the case, you perform as instructed. The ATM doesn't just give you $20, it will ask you what type of transaction you would like to make? The customer is in control; the customer dictates the services that the ATM provides. The same holds true for the salesperson in the new millennium.

The customer who comes to you most likely has a problem or need that she would like addressed. Remember the ATM? The only way you can offer additional information not originally requested by the customer is to query the customer. *Would you like to know more about how we can...?* The answer will be yes or no. If the customer says no, you don't tell him anyway. We are not suggesting you become robotic like an ATM. We are humans and building rapport should still be an objective for all salespeople. Based on the customer's needs as a result of your expert probes, provide the information the customer desires — no more and certainly no less.

TOP SECRET

You must become your customer's ATM — regardless of the products or services you sell.

43

LICENSE TO SELL

YOUR MISSION

Your mission is to think about the following questions as part of your intelligence gathering to capitalize on the *Applied Competency* trend.

❏ If you had to reduce your average sales call by 50%, what would you do?

_____
_____
_____

❏ What can you do to make your selling process more effective and efficient?

_____
_____
_____

❏ What would be the benefit(s) to the customer?

_____
_____
_____

❏ What would be the benefit to you?

_____
_____
_____

The 21st Century Salesperson

❏ What strategic closed probes (yes or no type response) could you use to uncover a customer need for your product or service? To get you thinking, complete the questions below:

Would you like to hear how we have helped customers like you save money with their x?

May I show you our x?

_____

_____

_____

_____

❏ Do you have a "bank" of strategically designed, close-ended questions readily available designed to get the customer to say yes to your presentation?

_____

_____

_____

❏ During a sales call with customers, what percentage of the time do you spend asking questions? Presenting information? Allowing the customer to talk? (total should = 100%)

_____

_____

_____

_____

_____

_____

LICENSE TO SELL

Perceptions of Trust & Credibility

Comfort levels and overall trust of the salesperson, the company and the transaction process will enter into the sales process due to the proliferation of electronic selling methods. Decisions will still be made based on facts — price, services, features, benefits, warranties, and guarantees — but more than ever, the decision will be based upon the perceptions of trust, comfort and credibility of you and your company.

The successful salesperson must answer key questions in the customer's mind:

- ✔ Who can I trust?
- ✔ Have I done business with this salesperson or company in the past?
- ✔ Did they do a good job?
- ✔ Can I trust them again?
- ✔ What if they don't perform as expected?
- ✔ What is my recourse?

TOP SECRET

If customers perceive they can get what they want, when they want it and know they can return it if it doesn't work — they will pay a little more for it if they can buy it from a company they can trust.

Doing business in the physical world one can see credibility and sense trust. Imagine a small, 1,000-square foot, locally owned and operated, hardware store next to a neat and clean, 60,000 square foot, new Home Depot. From the outside, which store has more credibility? Trust?

Now, let's move to the virtual world. Instantly, both stores become equal in size — limited only by the size of the customer's computer screen. The smaller local store now only has to create the perception of trust and credibility to compete against the huge competing chain store.

Just because you are the biggest and best in the physical world, doesn't mean it will translate into the virtual world. B. Dalton and Barnes & Noble have spent and continue to spend millions in physical retail locations. However, if I ask you to name a virtual bookstore, you would probably say amazon.com. What are you doing to become the virtual leader in your industry?

LICENSE TO SELL

YOUR MISSION

Your mission is to think about the following questions as part of your intelligence gathering to capitalize on the *Perceptions of Trust and Credibility* trend.

❏ What is your reputation in the industry with your customers?

_____
_____
_____
_____
_____
_____

❏ What brand names do you trust and buy from? Why?

_____
_____
_____
_____
_____
_____

❏ What can you do now to be perceived as trustworthy and credible?

_____
_____
_____
_____
_____

❏ How can you transfer that trust and credibility to a virtual environment?

❏ Does your web site look as trustworthy and credible as your biggest competitor? Why not? What can you do to bring yours up to speed? What can you do to bypass your competitors?

❏ List five customers you can contact to request a testimonial on customer service and support? How and where can you use the testimonials?

LICENSE TO SELL

The Salesperson as Orchestrator

Just as companies become virtual by using technology and outsourcing, so will salespeople who become more like symphony conductors or integrators. Their greatest skill will be their ability to meet the customers' needs by integrating the vendors, suppliers and information sources together in the quickest period of time. Their vision will become much more strategic than it is now. As orchestrators, salespeople will have to forecast and anticipate not just local changes, but also world changes and trends.

To make the big sale you may have to assemble a series of smaller sales. Some of those sales and interactions may even be with your competitors. Software sales is a perfect example of this trend. More often than not, the sale of one software solution may require the purchase, sale or coordination with competitors' software and services.

Your ability to present a solution that includes competitors' products and services, vendors outside of your company, or suppliers not in your immediate control is a selling trend that you must be prepared to meet.

> **TOP SECRET**
>
> *The greatest skill of new millennium salespeople will be their ability to meet the customers' needs by integrating the vendors, suppliers and information sources together in the quickest period of time.*

LICENSE TO SELL

YOUR MISSION

Your mission is to think about the following questions as part of your intelligence gathering to capitalize on the *The Salesperson as Orchestrator* trend.

❑ How well-read are you on the U.S. and global trends impacting your business?

_____
_____
_____

❑ What creative resources have you utilized to meet customers' needs?

_____
_____
_____

❑ What new or or additional resources would you need to develop to forecast and solve customers' needs?

_____
_____
_____

❑ What products and services, outside of those you provide, do you require to meet your customers' need? For example, do you ship via UPS or FedEx versus delivering products yourself? What other support services do you use?

_____
_____
_____

❏ In what instances are your competitor's products and services used in conjunction with yours?

_____
_____
_____

❏ Can you replicate or replace this overlap with products or services of your own? How? Can your competition replicate or replace your product or service? How?

_____
_____
_____

❏ When is it in the customer's best interest to use your competitor's products and services in conjunction with your own?

_____
_____
_____

❏ When is it in the customer's best interest for your competitors to use your products and services in conjunction with their own?

_____
_____
_____

❏ What can you do to enter into a strategic alliance with them in these instances?

_____
_____
_____

LICENSE TO SELL

SALES-EDGE TECHNOLOGY

Real-Time Selling

★

Remote Interaction with Customers

★

Virtual Storefronts

LICENSE TO SELL

Sales-Edge Technology

Real-Time Selling

Once a sales brochure or price sheet is printed, it's a dead document. Updating it may require reprinting the entire job, an often costly and time consuming process. The Internet has replaced a stagnant piece of information with real-time information that is alive — updated, corrected and instantly replaceable. This real-time information is available to both new and existing customers to view, print and use via your web site.

This concept not only applies to static information like rate sheets and brochures. Information in general — status reports, demonstrations, free trials, updates, price quotes — can be real-time information.

This real-time approach to doing business and moving information on an individual and customized basis has revolutionized the way we interact with one another. Company web sites, online banking, bill paying, video phones, smart cards and electronic cash are the ways we all will soon do business together. Real-time will also open up sales opportunities on a global basis. No longer will you have to physically be where the sale is made. Are you prepared for this opportunity?

> **TOP SECRET**
>
> *The concept of real-time selling doesn't only apply to static information like rate sheets and brochures. Information in general — status reports, updates, current situations — can be real-time information.*

57

LICENSE TO SELL

YOUR MISSION

Your mission is to think about the following questions as part of your intelligence gathering to capitalize on the *Real-Time Selling* trend.

❏ What real-time information can you provide to your customer via a web site, interactive voice mail, or other communications technology?

_____
_____
_____

❏ What percentage of material do you currently mail to your customers and prospects?

_____
_____
_____

❏ What documents/support material do you currently have in printed form?

_____
_____
_____

❏ What percentage of the material you listed above can and do you publish on the web?

_____
_____

❏ What benefits would you gain from pointing your customers and prospects to the web to get this information? Are there any drawbacks? If so, what can you do to minimize them?

_____
_____
_____

LICENSE TO SELL

Remote Interaction with Customers

As time moves forward, the concept of a field rep who physically visits customers will go the way of the manual typewriter. Computers, interactive videophones, the Internet, the telephone, e-mail, and other technology will eliminate many of the reasons for physically being onsite with the customer or prospect. At a minimum, it will change the reason and frequency for physically being onsite.

> **TOP SECRET**
>
> *Computers, interactive videophones, the Internet, the telephone, and other technology will eliminate the reason for physically being onsite. Or, at least change the reason and frequency for physically being onsite.*

LICENSE TO SELL

YOUR MISSION

Your mission is to think about the following questions as part of your intelligence gathering to capitalize on the *Remote Interaction with Customers* trend.

❏ What do you do currently to keep you and your company in front of your customers and prospects?

_____

_____

_____

❏ What is your competition doing?

_____

_____

_____

❏ To remotely stay in front of your customers, can you...

— publish a web-based or e-mail newsletter?

— advertise in the newspaper, on cable, on TV, or as a banner on a web site

— provide advertising specialties such as a computer mouse pad or coffee mug

— hyper-link your web site to a non-competing business (and theirs with yours) where their customers are your customers?

— sponsor an area sports team?

— send a birthday card?

— provide magnetic ads for the refrigerator, file cabinet, bumper, or car door?

❏ Does your web site look professional? Is it as good as one of your national competitors? Is it up to date? Can your customers view a "last updated" date right on the home page? Is it friendly? Is it two-way? Does it allow them to buy or transact business with you?

___

❏ Are you using toll-free numbers to develop and service your customer base?

___

❏ How can you use interactive voice mail to sell/service your customers and prospects?

___

LICENSE TO SELL

Virtual Storefronts

The Internet is transforming the way we do business. Soon, if not already, most simple sales or transactions will be done over the Internet by visiting a virtual storefront via a web site. Depending on the product, the delivery can be immediate such as downloading a new software program or overnight for receiving books, compact disks, food, and more.

Virtual retail shopping sidewalks are popping up all over the Internet. The interesting part of this paradigm is that none of the stores in the virtual mall need to exist physically. Retailers moving from the physical retail location to the virtual storefront include *amazon.com, buy.com, beyond.com, and sidewalk.com.* Just about anything that is sold at the local mall today will be, if it's not already, sold via the virtual mall of tomorrow.

TOP SECRET

A virtual company can change direction overnight by simply changing suppliers.

LICENSE TO SELL

YOUR MISSION

Your mission is to use the following questions as part of your intelligence gathering to capitalize on the *Virtual Storefront* trend.

❏ Do you have a web presence?

_____
_____
_____

❏ What is your competition doing? You can find out by using a search engine. Simply type in the category of products or services you sell and check out your competition. Visit the web sites that you find in the search results.

_____
_____
_____

❏ What do you like about your competitors' web sites?

_____
_____
_____

❏ What do you dislike about your competitors' web sites?

_____
_____
_____

❏ What could you do differently on your web site that would attract customers?

___

❏ If you already have a web site, did it show up in the search? How far down on the list of results were you? What can you do to increase your position in the search results?

___

LICENSE TO SELL

BETTER, FASTER & DIFFERENT SELLING STRATEGIES

Easy Access Business Profile

★

Virtual Companies

★

Branding and Electronic Cash

★

Upgrades and Enhancements

★

Partner with a Complimentary Company or Competitor

★

Defect Reduction

★

Selling Quality

LICENSE TO SELL

Better, Faster, Different Selling Strategies

Easy Access Business Profile

People have less time than ever before and literally every minute counts. The selling trend towards easily accessing businesses is based upon the fact in today's world "time is money."

The last thing customers want to do is spend their valuable time with a salesperson or company that can't offer quick easy sales or service. The longer it takes for your customer to do business with you, the more time and money you both lose. Conversely, the faster you can service customers, the happier they will be. Bottom line: it's in your best interest, and often the customer's, to complete the transaction as quickly and easily as possible.

Companies who make doing business easier and faster continue to gain market share. Drive-through windows once only seen at banks are everywhere from restaurants to convenience stores to dry cleaners. Mail order catalogs, the Internet, 800 numbers, 24-hour shopping, and shopping services are all designed to make access easier.

TOP SECRET

It's in your best interest to complete the transaction as quickly and easily as possible.

LICENSE TO SELL

YOUR MISSION

Your mission is to think about the following questions as part of your intelligence gathering to capitalize on the *Easy Access Business Profile* trend.

❏ On a scale of 1 to 7, with 7 being easiest, how easy is it for your customers to do business with you?

❏ In comparison to your competitors, where do you stand?

❏ What can you do to make doing business with you easier than doing business with your competitors?

❏ What do your customers want you to do differently? Survey a representative portion of your customer base and ask them.

Better, Faster, Different Selling Strategies

❏ In what ways can customers purchase your products today differently than they did five years ago?

_____

_____

_____

Next to each access item below, first note if it could work for your business, then identify on the scale how helpful it would be to your customers

Would Allow Customer Easy and Convenient Access to Product/Service

Yes	No		Not Help						Help
❏	❏	Drive-Through Window	1	2	3	4	5	6	7
❏	❏	24-Hour Access	1	2	3	4	5	6	7
❏	❏	Extended Hours	1	2	3	4	5	6	7
❏	❏	Drop Box	1	2	3	4	5	6	7
❏	❏	24-Hour Voice Mail	1	2	3	4	5	6	7
❏	❏	Mail-order Catalog	1	2	3	4	5	6	7
❏	❏	800 Phone Number	1	2	3	4	5	6	7
❏	❏	Accepting Credit Cards	1	2	3	4	5	6	7
❏	❏	Accepting Checks	1	2	3	4	5	6	7
❏	❏	Web Site w/Ordering	1	2	3	4	5	6	7
❏	❏	Free Delivery	1	2	3	4	5	6	7

❏ What else can you do to improve accessibility?

_____

_____

_____

LICENSE TO SELL

Better, Faster, Different Selling Strategies

Virtual Companies

Become the middleman. Good examples of this trend are computer manufacturers and bookstores. They have positioned themselves as the middlemen between buyer and manufacturer or wholesaler. If you want a computer, you call an 800 number. They ask your preferences for customization and quote a price. The price quoted is the wholesale price to build the machine plus a comfortable profit margin. They then take the order and outsource it to one of their suppliers who in turn builds the computer. The middleman then ships the computer with his logo to the customer.

Another example of this middleman position is amazon.com. They post the book on their web site. Upon receiving an order they either contact the publisher or pull the book from a small, on-hand inventory. Again, they pay wholesale for the book, charge retail to the customer and pocket the difference.

In essence they become a "virtual company," outsourcing every product or service they sell. This approach allows a company to be "in business" without the traditional overhead like manufacturing costs, labor, rent, etc. This is an amazing transformation that will allow many companies to literally become virtual. A virtual company can change direction overnight by simply changing suppliers. The old supplier is exchanged for the new who has the latest and greatest technology, services, products, cheapest labor force, etc. This limited or zero overhead turns into increased profits, competitive prices or both.

TOP SECRET

A virtual company can change direction overnight by simply changing suppliers.

LICENSE TO SELL

YOUR MISSION

Your mission is to think about the following questions as part of your intelligence gathering to capitalize on the *Virtual Companies* trend.

❏ If you could start over, how would you create a virtual company that sells the products or services you sell?

_____
_____
_____
_____
_____

❏ Does one exist now in your industry? How will you compete against it?

_____
_____
_____
_____
_____

❏ What manufacturing or services could you outsource?

_____
_____
_____
_____
_____

❏ What would be the advantages and disadvantages of outsourcing?

LICENSE TO SELL

Branding and Electronic Cash

Companies spend millions of dollars enhancing the image and trust of their products and services. Research shows customers will pay more for a brand that they know and trust versus one they have never heard of before. Companies leveraging this concept include Sears, Arm & Hammer, McDonalds, and Marriott International.

Trust-type companies and organizations such as banks are in a position to capitalize on this trust factor when it comes to payments. Since the name recognition and trust factor already exist, they can become the middlemen of doing business with no-name businesses.

Today, a customer paying by credit card versus cash has limited liability and possible recourse if the company he is buying from does not deliver. The bank is compensated for that "trust" factor in the form of a small percentage of commission from the sale. The business owner pays it out of his receipts for one primary reason. The sale may never have been made if he had to rely on a personal check.

What about cash? Cash works great if the buyer and seller are in the same physical location. But what about Internet sales? Cash will not work; credit cards work but there is no way for the business to verify a signature, picture ID, or gain an imprint of the card itself.

Back to the "trust" factor again. So, as a businessman, can you trust a customer you never met on the other end of a computer terminal? As a customer, can you trust a business that you found by surfing the web? The solution is trusting a third party both buyer and seller know, trust, and will guarantee the transaction.

Banks and other companies that are viewed as "trust" partners will be in a unique third party position to create and perpetuate the use of electronic cash. For a percentage of the transaction, they will bring trust to the electronic world of bill paying and presentment.

LICENSE TO SELL

YOUR MISSION

Your mission is to think about the following questions as part of your intelligence gathering to capitalize on the *Branding and Electronic Cash* trend.

❏ What is your company's reputation in the industry? Locally? Nationally? With employees? With customers?

_____
_____
_____
_____
_____

❏ How can you fully leverage your company's brand name? Do customers trust you? Why/why not?

_____
_____
_____
_____
_____

❏ What can you do to build trust in your company name?

_____
_____
_____
_____
_____

❏ What other products or services could you introduce or partner with that would bring enhanced trust to your product or service mix?

_____
_____
_____
_____
_____
_____
_____
_____
_____
_____
_____
_____

LICENSE TO SELL

Upgrades and Enhancements

Since the introduction of software, the concept of the product upgrade has moved from years to days. The new business attitude is to get it out the door first and fix any "bugs" in the next release or through the concept of a "patch." Think of a "patch" as a band-aid or fix to the problem. This aggressive philosophy is a result of pressure from several sides: worldwide competition, first-to-market, market share, embedding strategies, and customer demand. The days of waiting until you have crossed every "t" and dotted every "i" are over — at least for those companies wishing to stay in front of their competitors. This is a tremendous change and trend in our sales world.

In the software and computer business, upgrades are commonplace. We went from Microsoft DOS to Microsoft Windows 3.0 to 3.1 to 95 and 98, and there is no end in sight.

In the auto industry, you have a base model to which you can add options or upgrades. This approach allows the customer to customize the product to his exact needs. This also keeps the cost of the base model low — and competitive. The customer pays more for only those options of interest.

Could you significantly reduce the price of your product or service by creating a base model with an options pricing formula?

TOP SECRET

The new business attitude is to get it out the door first and fix any "bugs" in the next release.

LICENSE TO SELL

YOUR MISSION

Your mission is to think about the following questions as part of your intelligence gathering to capitalize on the *Upgrades and Enhancements* trend.

❑ What can you do to speed your product/service improvements to market?

_____
_____
_____
_____
_____

❑ How often do you release, upgrade, or enhance your products and services?

_____
_____
_____
_____
_____

❑ If you had to enhance your product/service every 180 days, how would you determine what enhancements to make?

_____
_____
_____
_____
_____

Better, Faster, Different Selling Strategies

❑ What have you done to overcome the drawbacks or "bugs" associated with your product or service?

___
___
___
___
___
___
___
___
___
___
___
___
___

LICENSE TO SELL

Partner with a Complementary Company or Competitor

Today's competitors may be tomorrow's partners. As we saw in the 80's and 90's one of fastest ways companies increased market share was to simply acquire their competitors and customers through mergers and acquisitions. This philosophy is prevalent in the banking, software and airline industries. The decision is a simple one: if it costs less to purchase the market share needed rather than go out and create it, you buy it.

While it still makes business sense to purchase competitors to gain market share, more companies will partner with firms that offer complementary products, services and resources to a qualified customer base. Partnering is a cost-effective alternative to the expense of carving out a customer base from an existing competitor market share. Federal Express did it with the U.S. Post Office and UPS. But can you? For most, partnering is the answer.

Through partnering, the parent company in many cases will share some of the assets and resources of one company with the other while keeping the companies, their brands and corporate identities separate. They may even share salespeople, customer databases and advertising materials as a way to leverage their existing sales.

In essence they become partners, understanding that it is in each of their best interests to work together rather than to work as separate entities. The best partners are those offering complementary services, products or resources to a like-minded customer base.

TOP SECRET

Partnering is a cost-effective alternative to carving out a customer base from an existing competitor market share. The best partners are those that offer complementary services, products or resources to one another.

The Internet has introduced a new form of partnering via hyperlinks and jump-site opportunities. Linking web sites and hyperlinked banner ads are just the beginning as this trend develops into jump-site leads, sales and commissions.

LICENSE TO SELL

YOUR MISSION

Your mission is to think about the following questions as part of your intelligence gathering to capitalize on the *Partner with a Complementary Company or Competitor* trend.

❏ What noncompetitors offer complementary products and services to a customer base similar to yours?

_____
_____
_____
_____
_____

❏ How would a partnership with each of these firms affect the sales of your products or services?

_____
_____
_____
_____
_____

❏ Who could you co-advertise with?

_____
_____
_____
_____
_____

Better, Faster, Different Selling Strategies

❏ What company's products could you co-sell (and vice-versa) with your own?

_____
_____
_____
_____
_____

❏ What company would you like to trade mailing lists for a special one-time mailing?

_____
_____
_____
_____
_____

LICENSE TO SELL

Defect Reduction

Successful companies must be quality oriented. Not to say this lightly, the big push these days is towards defect reduction. Many companies are striving towards reducing defects to less than 1%. The reason for this push is the tremendous competitive advantage it provides companies over their competitors. This is not an overnight process, and it is a tremendous commitment of time, money and behavioral changes. Those who adopt the process will reap the rewards.

The best example of defect reduction in action is the Japanese auto industry. In part, it is based on Edward Deming's 14 Points of Quality where anything and everything is benchmarked. Then the process is engineered and continuously reengineered with the goal of continuous improvement.

While the quality concept and defect reduction have been reserved for the manufacturing sectors, it is spreading to service-based organizations. Firms like Motorola, General Electric, Florida Power & Light, Ford, Cadillac, Citigroup, and Federal Express are all operating in this quality environment. Why? Fewer errors, defects and mistakes lead to greater productivity, increased customer satisfaction and higher revenue.

Think of defect reduction as the measurement of failures, defects or bad customer experiences. Most successful companies average about a 7% defect/error rate. In other words, seven out of every 100 experiences you have with a company may result in defects, failures or dissatisfaction.

A 7% defect rate would be disastrous for industries like the airlines, drinking water, drug prescriptions, and food manufacturers/packagers. As you can see some industries must operate at a reduced defect rate (less than 7%) capacity for them to survive and maintain customer trust. Most companies not dealing with life or death situations — and not actively measuring defects — can survive at 93% success rate. The ideal rate, of course, is 100% perfection. However, the cost of moving from 93% to 100% grows exponentially as you approach 100%. Consequently, every industry has a "trust" point or "acceptance" defect rate.

LICENSE TO SELL

YOUR MISSION

Your mission is to think about the following questions as part of your intelligence gathering to capitalize on the *Defect Reduction* and *Selling Quality* trends.

❑ What is your current defect rate?

___

❑ What is your company doing to reduce defects and improve its quality for customers?

___

❑ What is your competition doing?

___

❑ Could you sell quality and reliability? How?

___

❑ Can you outsource manufacturing, delivery or other services to firms that are 99% effective or have higher quality and fewer errors than you are able to produce in-house?

_____
_____
_____
_____

❑ What impact would that have on your sales? How could you leverage that when selling against the competition?

_____
_____
_____
_____

LICENSE TO SELL

Better, Faster, Different Selling Strategies

Selling Quality

What happens when companies start to apply the defect reduction concept to their non-life or death products and services to enhance customer satisfaction and reliability? As a salesperson, the company that can deliver quality (99.7% success) will have a tremendous competitive advantage over the company who is offering an error rate even just a few points less. The concept of quality as a whole will become a measure — a feature — the salesperson will use to sell you his product or service over the competitor's. For example, it will be an *"our quality or defect rate is better than theirs"* kind of comparison. This percent of defects concept will become so embedded into our culture that customers will begin to ask for it, incorporate it into business agreements and do business with only those willing to use such exacting measurements.

Consequently, knowing that many U.S. companies are quietly becoming quality-oriented, you must ask yourself what your firm is doing to reduce defects and improve its quality for its customers?

As mentioned, this is not an overnight improvement. It can take years and millions of dollars of reinvestment in a company to make it happen. Even more so, one way many companies will catch up on their quality is to outsource manufacturing, delivery and services to firms that have already embedded a quality ethic and statistical measurement process. After all, it will be less expensive in the long run to outsource work that can be performed at 99.7% accuracy, than pay for the inhouse mistakes and rework of an accuracy rate of 93% or less.

> **TOP SECRET**
>
> *The way many companies will catch up with defect reduction is to outsource manufacturing, delivery and services to firms with better defect reduction methods.*

LICENSE TO SELL

SALES SKILLS

Sales Skills are organized in three major sections:

> *—Before the Sale*
>
> *—During the Sale*
>
> *—After the Sale*

Remember, sales is not a concrete activity. There will be overlap and a blending of skills to achieve your goals.

LICENSE TO SELL

Before the Sale   **SALES SKILLS**

Prospecting 101 and Beyond

One of the main reasons businesses fail is that they don't spend enough time and resources prospecting for new business. The same goes for the success of salespeople. For many sales professionals, "The toughest door to open is your own!" You have got to get out of the office and call on prospects; the absolute *minimum* amount of time should be 20% or one day per week.

What do we mean by prospecting? It is a combination of networking and meeting with prospects in their environment. People will say, "It is impossible for me to get out of the office or operation." If you don't have time, pay someone to do it for you! Hire an hourly telemarketer or a direct mail house. No matter what your business, you need to find customers. Once you have done your research about *who* would want to buy from you, you've got to get out there and meet *them*.

Cost of a Sales Call. Do you know the approximate cost of a sales call for your organization? Try this simple formula. Divide the total annual sales income by the total number of actual calls that produce a sale which equals the cost of your average sales call.

$$\$1{,}000{,}000 \div 2{,}000 = \$500$$

Now you do it!

_____ ÷ _____ = _____

(your annual sales income)   (# of actual calls that produce a sale)   (average sales revenue per call)

Note: Your goal is to make the average sales revenue per call larger. You want to go on fewer calls and make more money.

Look at that cost and realize how important it is to try and avoid calls to prospects who have limited potential.

LICENSE TO SELL

A huge "given" in the world of sales is: TO KEEP YOUR JOB, YOU HAVE TO BEAT YOUR SALES GOALS. Many people miss their sales goals because they do not know where to find prospects and quickly qualify them.

Where do you begin to find prospects for your product/service? If your company has a history, your research begins with past and current customers. An existing database will give you keen insight to the types of customers likely to buy in the future.

Past Customers. There are many reasons why customers stop doing business with you:
- ✔ A customer can move from the area;
- ✔ A customer can get a better deal from a competitor;
- ✔ A company can go out of business;
- ✔ A company can be purchased by a larger company;
- ✔ The main buyer in a company can leave and his replacement could have a preference for another product/service;
- ✔ A customer may only have a one-time use or her needs have changed perhaps due to new technology.

Think about your own buying habits. You shop, dine and gas up your car at convenient, enjoyable places. The places you frequent today have probably not always been your favorites. Something occurred that caused you to have a new favorite spot to shop or eat in. How would you respond if you got a phone call that went like this:

"Ms. _____, we know you used to be a regular customer, but you have not been in for months. Did we do something wrong? What can we do to earn you back as a customer?"

That type of call would knock me out! I wouldn't care if it came from a dry cleaner, restaurant or hair stylist. It would give me a chance to tell them the real reason why they haven't seen me for a while.

Contact your former customers to find out:

1) What made them buy in the first place?

2) What or who is getting their business now instead of you? And most importantly why?

These answers will give you a keen insight into who your competition is. You will also have the chance to ask some magical questions like:

What could I do to get you to try us again?

Face it, they liked you enough to buy from you in the past, so why not rekindle that customer?

Another important group of customers are those who have left you. Again, contact them and ask them why they no longer do business with you. This will provide you with strategic information you need to know to fix your problem before it's too late.

You should rank the reasons why your customers left. Addressing the top one or two reasons will often save as much as 80% of the customers who you've lost in the past.

Can you think of a few past customers you have not seen or spoken to for a while? List two or three below and a date to follow-up with them.

1. _____ Date: _____ Result: _____
2. _____ Date: _____ Result: _____
3. _____ Date: _____ Result: _____

Current Customers. Customers currently doing business with you are the most important group to research. They can be a source to buy from you again, as well as an excellent source for referrals. Who better to call on and ask for referrals, testimonials or more business than current satisfied customers? They already know about your product/service and you know about them — including their credit history. A careful analysis of current customers can be used to build a profile of the ideal prospect.

Do not abuse this privilege. Customers will respect your approach once they understand that you are trying to expand a market and could use their advice on potential customers.

LICENSE TO SELL

Your Mission

Make a list of three current customers to call and choose a date to call on them.

1. _____ Date: _____

Primary reason why they do/don't do business with you:

_____

_____

2. _____ Date: _____

Primary reason why they do/don't do business with you:

_____

_____

3. _____ Date: _____

Primary reason why they do/don't do business with you:

_____

_____

Secret Message

Be sure and recognize your current customer with a handwritten thank you for the referral. Occasionally, notify them of how you are progressing with the referral. Customers usually have an interest in knowing "the rest of the story." They may be able to give you some valuable coaching tips along the way depending on how well they know the referral. To truly standout in a customer's eyes, send *them* a referral! As a matter of fact, send them *two* so the customer will feel they owe you one!

Before the Sale   **SALES SKILLS**

Prospecting for New Customers

New prospects are all around you. Here are some resources to find them:

- ✔ Referrals from customers
- ✔ Educational seminars you sponsor or attend
- ✔ Friends and family
- ✔ Industry-specific trade shows
- ✔ Trade publications/magazines
- ✔ Web sites
- ✔ Database marketing lists (mail and telephone)
- ✔ Cold call canvassing
- ✔ Dunn & Bradstreet leads
- ✔ Newspaper articles
- ✔ Yellow pages
- ✔ Chamber of Commerce members
- ✔ Networking lead share groups
- ✔ Lateral selling within an organization
- ✔ Fax broadcasts
- ✔ Bulk e-mail
- ✔ Classified ads
- ✔ Reverse trade show marketing
- ✔ Signs and ads
- ✔ Circle of influence direct mail letters

You will increase your sales opportunities by keenly listening to past and current customers. They have valuable knowledge to impart if you are willing to listen and learn.

LICENSE TO SELL

Your Mission

Out of the 20 sources listed, pick the top 4 for your market. Then write a mission to apply these sources on the job.

1. _____
_____
_____

2. _____
_____
_____

3. _____
_____
_____

4. _____
_____
_____

You need to prospect and network where you are most likely to find potential customers. Make a list of current business organizations of which you are a member:

_____
_____
_____

Make a list of organizations of which your customers are members:

_____
_____
_____
_____

Are there organizations on your customer's list and not on yours? If so, the organization may be an excellent place to prospect. The beauty of being out there rubbing elbows and shaking hands is that you get to talk with strangers who may be your future customers. Take advantage of this opportunity to tell people what you do. Think about it this way — you are only three people away from knowing key decision makers. You can meet somebody who knows the decision maker you need to meet.

The 30-Second Commercial. Before you come in contact with your next prospect, try this exercise:

You have no more than 30 seconds to capture someone's attention. Don't waste a word by giving someone your title or your company. Separate yourself from others by telling people about the **results** they can expect by buying your product or service. For example:

"I help people dramatically improve their selling skills by sharpening their listening skills with a unique training program I developed."

Your Mission

Write out a 15-30 second commercial for yourself telling people about the results they can expect from your product or service.

_____
_____
_____
_____
_____
_____
_____

LICENSE TO SELL

Before the Sale   **SALES SKILLS**

The Art of Asking Questions — an Open and Closed Case

In order for us to get prospects to start talking, they usually need to be directed with questions. If you want to learn more about prospects, you'll need to plan a series of questions. You probably know the two main types of questions or probes are "open" and "close-ended."

Open Probes. An open-ended probe is used to obtain additional information from the customer. It's characterized by a few key words that force the prospect to elaborate on her answers so you can learn more about her needs. The question will require more than a simple yes or no response. This allows you to maximize time and effectiveness of the sales call. It also helps you to clarify and confirm needs, identify potential opportunities for business, build relationships, and illustrate your professionalism, competence, and expertise.

To get prospects talking, an open-ended question usually starts off with the classic open probe words: who, what, where, why, when, how, tell. Such as:

- ✔ *Tell me about your...*
- ✔ *How would you respond...*
- ✔ *How can we make sure...*
- ✔ *Why does your company...*
- ✔ *Tell me how the final decision...*
- ✔ *What is the difference between...*
- ✔ *What do you look for in choosing...*
- ✔ *What if I proposed...*
- ✔ *Tell me who in your organization...*

LICENSE TO SELL

Asking open-ended questions is the first step in rapport building. Open-ended questions get the customer talking and you listening and taking notes.

By getting the customer to open up, you allow him to reveal opportunity areas where your product or service may be of value. This background information allows you to custom fit a presentation using the customer's information rather than a generic, scripted one.

Your Mission

Think of a prospect you are currently working with. List at least two open-ended questions you would like to ask during your next appointment:

1. _____
_____

2. _____
_____

Closed Probes. A close-ended probe is used to confirm customer information. Close-ended questions are also characterized by a few key words and are useful when obtaining or confirming specific information or knowledge. The classic close-ended probes start with: is, are, does, do, did, have, would.

It can usually be answered in a simple "yes" or "no" response:

✔ *Would you agree...*

✔ *Is it fair to say...*

✔ *Have you spoken to...*

✔ *Did you know..*

✔ *Is it true that...*

✔ *So what you need is...*

Before the Sale **SALES SKILLS**

- ✔ *Do you have...*
- ✔ *Does it matter...*
- ✔ *So what you are looking for is...*
- ✔ *Are you aware...*

Unlike open probes that are rapport makers, closed probes are rapport breakers! Try to have a lively conversation with someone by only asking closed probes. What you end up with is an interrogation!

Secret Message. Have a balance of open and close-ended questions prepared. Ask more open than closed and listen carefully to the answers. You will be amazed what prospects will tell you — if you'll just ask and listen!

Your Mission

Now, think about a current prospect and list two close-ended questions you would like to ask during your next appointment:

1. _____

_____

2. _____

_____

Next to each key word, write a question that leads off with the word designed to uncover a need for your product or service:

Open-ended Probes

Who _____

What _____

109

LICENSE TO SELL

Why _____

Where _____

When _____

How _____

Tell me _____

Close-Ended Probes

Is _____

Are _____

Does _____

Do _____

Did _____

Have _____

Would _____

Before the Sale   **SALES SKILLS**

Qualifying — It's All in the Questions

Remember, you are selling while you are LISTENING! The use of effective questioning techniques that qualify prospects has become a lost art! Preparing the right questions and using active listening skills coupled with PATIENCE is the key to proper qualifying. You will want to ask questions designed to reveal the prospect's needs and problems.

In qualifying, you are trying to answer three basic questions for yourself:

- ✔ Does a need exist?
- ✔ Are you talking to the decision maker or at least someone who has influence with the final decision maker?
- ✔ Do they have the resources (cash, credit) to buy?

Trap to Avoid! Do not jump on the first hint of a need or problem and begin selling. It is very tempting to do that when you first hear someone describe a problem that you can fix. We can't stress this enough — you are selling while you are listening! The goal in qualifying is to discover and prioritize ALL the needs and problems BEFORE you attempt to help solve them. BE PATIENT!

At this stage, you are playing the role of a problem solver. You should not present solutions until at least one primary need has surfaced and have confirmed that no other primary needs exist.

To confirm that no additional primary needs exist you might ask an open probe like:

What else would you like to improve if given the chance?

Or, ask a closed probe like:

Many of our customers who used the product you are using now found _____ to be a problem — is it a problem for you?

111

LICENSE TO SELL

Key Words. Customers will often contact you when they have a need for your product or service. Key words to listen for include:

- ✔ solution
- ✔ wish
- ✔ need
- ✔ looking for
- ✔ want
- ✔ interested in
- ✔ like
- ✔ important to me

Key Phrases. You might hear the following phrases while listening to a customer. In essence, the prospect is qualifying herself:

- ✔ *The solution to my problem...*
- ✔ *What our company needs is...*
- ✔ *I want a way to...*
- ✔ *I would like to have...*
- ✔ *I wish there was a way to...*
- ✔ *I'm looking for...*
- ✔ *What is important to me is...*

Sometimes when a customer contacts you, they have a solution in mind and know what they want. Unfortunately, this is the exception and not the norm. Most customers tend to talk in terms of opportunities or problems.

An Opportunity to Probe. By definition, an opportunity or problem is a customer's problem that your product or service can fix. Unlike customers' needs or solutions, opportunities are not clear-cut statements stating a desire to solve the problem at hand. Problems are most likely revealed in the form of negative statements or complaints about the customer's current situation.

Before the Sale SALES SKILLS

Problems are also not revealed as a result of the customer using "key" words or phrases. While needs and solutions are expressed as a customer's want or desire to solve a problem, opportunities are everything else. Basically, if there's not a clear need for your product or service, then it should be treated as an opportunity.

Your Mission

As you read the following statements, notice the difference between customer problems and customer needs. Put a "N" next to the statements you feel are needs and an "O" next to those you feel are opportunities. For this exercise, pretend the features and benefits of your product or service *can* satisfy the following needs and opportunities.

_____ My current car eats gas; it only gets 12 miles per gallon.

_____ I want a car that gets good gas mileage.

_____ Our current invoice is difficult to read.

_____ I need an invoice that is easy to read.

_____ I'm looking for a way to improve productivity.

_____ Currently productivity is down.

Answers: O,N,O,N,O,N.

Sample Qualifying Questions. Here are some sample qualifying questions to use:

✔ What is your objective?

✔ What problems are you experiencing?

✔ How are you handling those problems today?

✔ What has been your experience?

✔ Are you the decision-maker?

✔ What do you see as the solution?

✔ So you're looking for a way to....?

✔ What can you tell me about the success and failures of past vendors?

LICENSE TO SELL

✔ Assuming a solution is identified, is paying for it all an issue that needs to be addressed?

✔ Does this company/prospect have a need for my product or service? If yes, continue; if no, move on.

✔ Do they have the resources or arrangements to pay? If not move on.

Prioritizing Your Unique Strengths. Make sure that you take notes while the prospect is answering your qualifying questions. Continue the process after each need is described by asking, *"Are there any additional needs you have?"* Once you have a list of needs confirm. Say, *"Let me review all the needs I have heard so far."* When the prospect agrees that covers them, if not obvious ask, *"How would you prioritize these needs from most important to least important?"* By getting the answer to that question, you will know the order in which to sell your unique strengths. It's also helpful if you have to negotiate later.

Up until now, what you have sold is: yourself, your consultative approach to the problem, and a sincere interest in learning about the prospect's needs. You have built the right foundation for the custom presentation (based solely on the needs uncovered) that will soon follow.

Before the Sale   **SALES SKILLS**

Outbound Telemarketing is Proactive

The telephone is one of the sales professional's most effective prospecting and selling tools, especially when it's used with outbound telemarketing. Telemarketing may be one of the best ways to identify the most number of qualified prospects in the shortest period of time. But unlike traditional telemarketers who read from a script, you must become a pro and anticipate and be prepared for a hostile, indifferent and skeptical customer. Knowing how to penetrate these negative customer attitudes over the phone will provide you with a much better chance of obtaining customer interest.

Selling by Phone. The secret to selling by phone is the same as selling on a street corner. Wouldn't you agree that customers hate being telemarketed? Wouldn't you agree they are likely to hang up on you in the first 10 seconds or so? Knowing this, the question to ask is a simple one that requires a yes or no type answer.

The secret is to develop a question that will give you the answer you are looking for — yes or no. For example:

"If there was a way to reduce your current long distance expenses by 50% — guaranteed — would you be interested in receiving some free information in the mail?"

The customer who is interested will respond "yes" and you are on your way to the next question.

Knowing the customer will likely want to give you a "no" response and that he will be guarding against any kind of "yes" answer, you may want to develop a closed ended probe that will allow the customer to respond "no," such as:

"You wouldn't knowingly and willingly pay up to 50% more for a long distance call if you didn't have to, would you?"

Assuming the customer says no, you might continue with,

115

LICENSE TO SELL

"Then it stands to reason if there was a way to reduce your current cost of long distance calls by 50% you would be interested in learning more, true?"

Does this sound sound like a lawyer cross-examining a witness? If you said yes, you're right. However, keep in mind the tone of your voice must take any aggressiveness out of the questions. Good salespeople are consultative. They ask questions and never assume that what they have to sell will satisfy the customer's needs 100%, at least in the beginning.

Window of Opportunity. Think of that initial interaction with the customer as a window of opportunity. Sometimes that window of opportunity is open wide and even the most novice of salespeople could pass through it. But most windows will appear closed to most salespeople. Good salespeople will find a crack in the window somewhere. Because the crack is not big enough to pass through they must use closed probes as a wedge to leverage the window open wider and wider to a point where they can pass through.

80-20 Sales Rule. Remember if 80% of the windows of opportunity you try to pass through slam shut on you, you are a success. Let's state it again, if 80% of the windows of opportunity you try to pass through slam shut on you, you are a success. Sales is a numbers game. In other words, 80% of the windows slam shut, that means you were able to penetrate 20% and make a sale. That's a 20% close ratio. For most salespeople a 20% close ratio translates into a good living, and with practice, it only gets better.

Your Mission

Imagine you were on a busy street corner and you only could ask one question to gain customer interest (a yes response) in your product or service. Write three questions you could ask:

_____

_____

_____

Before the Sale   **SALES SKILLS**

Gatekeepers & Voice Mail

What are the chances of getting to speak to a key decision maker in today's business environment on your first call? Chances are you'll either encounter an assistant or voice mail. Here are several effective techniques to make interactions with receptionists and voice mail work to your advantage.

Gatekeepers. Realize that a company's main receptionist can be one of your allies. Suppose you are trying to reach a company's purchasing department, but you do not have a name. Ask the operator who answers the phone for the head of purchasing's name, as well as his secretary's name. Chances are if you don't get voice mail, you'll get a secretary. If by chance you do get to speak to the person you are looking for, be prepared with your 30-second commercial.

Example

Here is a sample phone conversation with a gatekeeper:

Is this Rose? Rose, my name is Doug Price and I understand you are the assistant to _____, the head of purchasing - is that right? I respect your time very much so I will be brief. Rose, the purpose of my call is that ultimately, I would like to see your boss and explain the benefits of my product / service. Is your boss the person who would make that sort of buying decision for the company? Great. I would like to get some information in front of (the boss). I will be sending information (via fax, mail, or E-mail) <u>to your attention</u>. Would you be kind enough to pass it along to him? I will follow-up with you to ensure it arrived and that your boss has had a chance to see it. Then, I'd like your help in arranging for either a phone or face-to-face appointment. Can I count on you?

LICENSE TO SELL

The purpose of winning over gatekeepers is that they can assist you in gaining access to the ultimate decision maker. They might also be in a position to put in a good word for you when you really need it.

On the day you arrive for your meeting, it is strongly recommended that you do something nice for gatekeepers to thank them for helping you secure the appointment. You usually will score high with chocolates of some sort! Better yet, have chocolates with your company logo made up. It will make quite an impression.

Secret Message. In many small businesses, the gatekeeper is often a relative or immediate family member — so be nice to everyone!

Using the Gatekeeper for Research. Getting lucky in sales is not easy. You need to plan a series of calls to gain knowledge before you go on your appointment call, or your luck may run out after your first call!

Your objective is to find out all you can about the prospective customer and his organization, so you will be organized and display a compelling interest. Here's how you can obtain information on your prospective customer by using the gatekeeper:

✔ Call the gatekeeper and explain how you are attempting to do research to uncover information that will make your call with her boss more efficient and effective.

Questions you may want to ask the gatekeeper include:

✔ How long has your boss been in this current job?

✔ How many years has your boss worked with the organization and what other places and jobs has he held?

✔ Any family particulars that would help (e.g. spouse, kids, pets). This is a good time to see if the gatekeeper will reveal the boss's birthday. It might be coming up and people usually enjoy getting cards on their birthday!

Before the Sale   **SALES SKILLS**

- ✔ Ask if the department is currently working on any large scale projects that are time-consuming.
- ✔ Inquire about current issues the department or the company is currently facing.
- ✔ Get knowledge about any vendors that you could compete with.
- ✔ Ask about the chain of command or organizational structure to see where the boss fits in the organization's hierarchy.
- ✔ Learn what the boss's schedule looks like prior to and after your scheduled appointment. This will give you an indication of the person's time commitments and what their day may be like.

Organizational Info. Here's how to obtain information on the organization:

- ✔ Talk with the gatekeeper or anyone you may know in the organization.
- ✔ Find out the web site address and spend time studying it.
- ✔ Check the Internet for articles on industry trends that would be relevant for your discussion.
- ✔ Locate a copy of an annual report if applicable.
- ✔ Check the library for articles on the company that may have appeared in newspapers, magazines and trade journals.

Secret Message. To maximize your chances of a successful appointment, do your pre-work and be prepared to demonstrate your interest in both the organization and the prospect. Have an objective for the call that is measurable and achievable during the appointment. It may be to simply fill in the knowledge gaps that exist as a result of your pre-work calls!

LICENSE TO SELL

Your Mission

Make a list of at least three gatekeepers who present a challenge to you. Your mission is to develop a strategy to "win them over" to your side.

_____
_____
_____
_____
_____
_____
_____

What questions could you ask the gatekeeper that provide you with the most information about your customer prior to the actual sales call.

_____
_____
_____
_____
_____
_____
_____
_____
_____
_____
_____

Voice Mail — Better Known as Voice Jail. Voice mail has changed the business landscape almost as dramatically as e-mail. Though it can be an asset, too many use their voice mail to hide from salespeople!

With voice mail, listen carefully to the other person's message. If it is an up-to-date message, you can learn about their schedule for the day or week. It will give you a good opportunity to use what you learned when it is your turn to leave a message. Here are some tips on how to manage another person's voice mail message:

- ✔ Speak s-l-o-w-l-y and directly into the mouthpiece of the phone.
- ✔ Spell your name right away and slowly give your phone number immediately and again at the end.
- ✔ Listen to the voice mail message and determine if it gives insight as to the person's whereabouts.
- ✔ Leave a brief but complete message as to why you are calling.

Message Formula. A formula to keep in mind when leaving messages is:

- ✔ Be friendly
- ✔ Show respect
- ✔ Be brief, but speak slowly
- ✔ State your purpose

Example of an effective voice mail message:

This is (your name) (N-A-M-E) of (company). My phone is (number). I will be brief since you may be listening to this while you are traveling. Your voice mail indicates you will be back in your office Friday. I am going to be sending information to your office describing myself and my company. I give talks on Listening and Selling Skills, and I would like to talk to you about a speaking arrangement with your firm. You do not need to call me from the road — unless you would like to! If we have not spoken by next Tuesday, (date), I will call you to speak further.

LICENSE TO SELL

Once again, my name is (your name) and my phone number is (your phone number). Thank you for your valuable time listening to this message.

Voice Mail Works Both Ways. Now, think of your voice mail message from the other side of the phone. How do those who call you perceive your voice mail message? The other aspect of managing voice mail is the impression you want to make on your callers while away from the phone. Your message should:

- ✔ Convey your whereabouts and tell callers when they can expect to hear from you.
- ✔ Convey an upbeat, friendly and informative message.
- ✔ Convey to the callers how to get to a real person if necessary.
- ✔ Convey when callers can expect a return call from you.
- ✔ Be changed daily, and if out for more than one day, have your message reflect the length of time you'll be away.
- ✔ Be spoken slowly and directly into the mouthpiece.

Basically, what customers want to know is how to get help if needed and/or when they can expect to hear back from you.

Example message:

"Hi, this is (your name) at (your company). Monday, January 5, I will be out of the office until 2:00. I will return your call between 2:00 and 5:00 P.M. today. If you need immediate assistance, press 0 and speak to my assistant Sarah. Thank you for your call and I look forward to speaking with you soon."

After you record your daily message, play it back and listen to it. Be critical and ask yourself:

- ✔ Is my tone of voice upbeat and friendly?
- ✔ Is the message clear or too fast?

If you feel as though the message can somehow be improved, rerecord the message! Remember, this is the first impression you may be giving a prospect. Do your best to convey sincerity and your willingness to get back to them in a timely fashion.

Before the Sale   **SALES SKILLS**

Your Mission

Write down your current office voice mail message. How can you improve upon it?

LICENSE TO SELL

Before the Sale   **SALES SKILLS**

The Sales Cycle

Every product or service has a sales cycle associated with it. A sales cycle is simply the amount of time or number of calls typically required from the moment a potential customer or prospect is identified to the moment he or she accepts delivery or assumes ownership of your product or service. For the most part, the greater the item (the more it costs), the longer the sales cycle.

If I need to buy a can of paint for my house, I go off to the store and return with a can of paint. I don't need to review the purchase with my accountant or attorney and get their signatures or approval.

On the other hand, if I was going to purchase paint to have my maintenance staff paint the interior of my company's office building — all 32 floors including the stairwells — the sales cycle is a little different. I would probably meet with a paint salesperson, who would probably come to me as opposed to me going to him. There would most likely be some kind of a discount due to the volume of paint, and therefore some kind of negotiation process would be required. Given the dollars involved, there would also probably be a written agreement that would specify the number of gallons of paint, color, brand, price and delivery date. Consequently, attorneys would be involved and they would require a round of contract comments and revisions. Finally, there would have to be some way of delivering the paint. The delivery time and location would have to be agreed upon and coincide with my painter's schedule. As you can see this process or sales cycle is a little longer and more complex than going to the local hardware store and buying a gallon of paint.

Secret Message. Understanding your sales cycle will help you determine the type of close or the action you want the customer to take each time you communicate with the customer. In a short, a one-call sales cycle, your close may involve asking the customer to purchase, sign, pay, buy, take, demo, use, or agree to whatever it is you are selling.

LICENSE TO SELL

In a long or multicall sales cycle, your close will be determined by the phase of the sales cycle you are in at the time. When you first meet a customer, your close may simply be to get the customer to agree to a second meeting so you can make a formal presentation. At the second call, your next close may be to get the customer to agree to accept or review a written proposal. The sales call after that might involve the ultimate or final close designed to get the customer's approval or to sign the proposal and give you a deposit thereby closing the sale.

Your Sales Cycle. Here's how you can determine your sales cycle by following these easy steps:

1) Determine the end point of your sale. Is it a signed contract? A delivery? A payment? Use the space on page 128.

2) Determine the starting point of your sales process. When do you first make contact with the customer? Is it by phone? Is it in person? Is it by mail? Again, use the space on page 128.

3) Determine where the middle point is; when are you halfway through the process? Is it a presentation? Is it a demonstration? Is the presentation of a proposal? Use the space on page 128.

Now take a moment to fill in all the steps — customer contact points — between the first step and the halfway point. Do the same and identify all the steps — customer contact points — from the halfway point to the last step.

4). Number the total steps in the process. You may have three, five, ten maybe even 20 or more.

5) Looking at each of the steps in your sales cycle, what kind of customer commitment or action are you asking for at each step in your sales cycle?. Write it down to the right of each step in your sales cycle on page 128.

Having this information allows you to not only plan your call, but also have an objective. Sometimes in the very first sales call the customer wants the process to move quickly and is ready to buy or close. So be careful you don't undersell or cause your sales cycle steps and outcomes to limit you in any way. They may all occur during the same call or just in one step of the sales cycle. If the customer is ready to sign the agreement and write you a check, you don't say, *"wait a minute I haven't given you a demonstration yet or typed up a formal proposal."* Be a good closer and fast-forward through your sales cycle objectives and get the sale.

The sales cycle is a road map for you, as well as your sales manager, to use to determine where you are in the sale at any given time. It gives you perspective on when you're moving fast. It allows you to anticipate how much time is left before the close, thus allowing you to prepare or position your closing statements with the customer.

LICENSE TO SELL

Starting Point of the Sales Cycle:	Customer Commitment or Action
Middle Point of the Sales Cycle:	
End Point of the Sales Cycle:	

During the Sale   **SALES SKILLS**

Relationship Building: YOU are the Initial Product

Unless you are fortunate enough to be selling Rolls Royce automobiles, you need to sell yourself, as well as your product, service or company. Think about this — your name and what it stands for are the most important words in any language. When it is spoken or written, you will usually acknowledge it in some way.

Comfort Factor. People do not care how much you know — until they know how much you care. People buy from people they feel comfortable with. The very first thing you need to be selling to prospective customers is yourself. It is usually the feature the customer knows the least about, but ultimately will buy.

In this fast-paced world we live in, you need to respect people's time. On a first-time call, your sales objective should be to get to know your prospective customer. Take the time to get better acquainted; use the first five minutes of the call, if appropriate.

Face-to-Face. Just by looking around the office walls or at the desk, you may get a clue about areas of interest. It is normally safe to comment on something in the customer's office. Be careful not to boast about your own interest or talents that would minimize the accomplishments of the prospective customer.

Build a Bridge. Think about ways to bridge a conversation by having one point lead into another. For instance, if you sell copiers for a living, you might tell a story about a customer who purchased a machine last month and is writing off a portion of it to a nonprofit group. You might add that you know the person is making flyers for his kids upcoming soccer tournament. Then ask, *"Do you have kids?"* Build a bridge to talk about what you may have in common with kids.

LICENSE TO SELL

Secret Message. The reason for building rapport is that it makes it harder for the customer to say "no" to someone they know or like! Remember, the salesperson's purpose of the call is NOT ONLY to qualify the prospect, but also to build and create a relationship.

Talking Business. If you're wondering when to stop the "small talk" and start talking business, here's a sample script that you can try with your next prospective customer:

"Thank you for seeing me today. I respect your time and only want to borrow about five minutes. If I am here longer than five minutes, it is because you want me to be here. One of my objectives is to get to know you better as well as your company and needs. With your permission, I would like to begin with a few background questions. OK?"

This makes it easy for the customer to say yes because you have only asked for five minutes, and the customer gets to say whether to continue or not.

Be sure to write down what they want to accomplish and repeat it back to them. Make certain that you do accomplish what the prospect expects! You should agree on what you both feel can be accomplished in the allotted time.

Also, when the prospect hears you ask questions designed to get to know them better, they won't wonder why you are asking these questions. You told them up front that getting to know them is one of your objectives! Once the prospective customer begins to smile, use your name, give longer answers to your questions, and use positive body language, you will know rapport has been established and it is time to get down to business!

During the Sale   **SALES SKILLS**

Your Mission

You can use the following topics to quickly build rapport:

Geography — *Where are you calling from?* Follow up with a comment whether the customer is local or from out of town.

History — *Has your organization bought from us?* Yes, this is a qualifying question, but it can also be used to build rapport by building on the answer.

Weather — It is common to talk weather, particularly if there is something significant occurring.

News — Ask about positive news events that may affect the customer or current general business news headlines.

Write out 2-3 rapport-building topics you're comfortable using:

Over the phone:

_____

_____

_____

Face to face:

_____

_____

_____

LICENSE TO SELL

During the Sale   **SALES SKILLS**

Customer Traits

Your ability to read people and adapt your selling style accordingly will take you a long way in sales. Some of the best salespeople are those who can adapt to a variety of customers. They know how to connect, how to phrase words and sentences so they will most likely be accepted by the customer. Sometimes the same customer will go through a series of emotions during a single call requiring you to adapt minute by minute.

Here are some general customer traits and strategies to effectively interact with these types of customers.

The Driver/Decision Maker

✔ likes to be in control

✔ wants respect

✔ likes admiration

✔ serious, sometimes rigid thinking

✔ aggressive and demanding

✔ likes logic

✔ interested in end results

✔ organized

How to handle:

✔ let her do the talking, run the call

✔ ask direct questions

✔ compliment him

✔ acknowledge her comments

✔ stick to the facts

✔ build a case

✔ talk in terms of end results

✔ stick to business

133

LICENSE TO SELL

The Socializer
- ✔ wants to be liked
- ✔ friendly
- ✔ talkative
- ✔ likes recognition
- ✔ likes to associate with others
- ✔ shares personal stories
- ✔ good sense of humor

How to handle:
- ✔ build a relationship
- ✔ talk about the benefits to the group
- ✔ be friendly
- ✔ tell client-oriented stories
- ✔ share personal information about yourself
- ✔ build trust
- ✔ tell a funny joke

Mr./Ms. Play It Safe
- ✔ high safety needs
- ✔ doesn't like risk
- ✔ likes to think about it
- ✔ likes to get others' opinions
- ✔ indecisive
- ✔ passive in nature

During the Sale **SALES SKILLS**

How to handle:

✔ go slow with your presentation

✔ pause to assure complete understanding and comfort along the way

✔ stress the benefits that promote safety or minimal risk

✔ ask her questions she can agree with

The Politician

✔ wants to make everyone happy

✔ likes to negotiate

✔ will say yes but not mean it

✔ non-committal

✔ likes to play games

✔ keeps changing the deliverables

✔ not genuine

How to handle:

✔ define expectations and deliverables before talking price

✔ ask alternative choice type questions

✔ be careful of games

✔ make sure he is qualified before presenting

LICENSE TO SELL

Your Mission

List five current or prospective customers and identify their personality style. Now, think about your next opportunity to meet this person. What can you do to effectively meet the customer's personality style?

_____

_____

_____

_____

_____

_____

_____

_____

How would you label your own traits when you are a customer?

_____

_____

_____

How do you like to be handled by a salesperson?

_____

_____

_____

Benefit Selling: Transitioning from Features to Tactical Benefits

Features don't sell a customer; benefits do. You don't buy a four-door car because it has four doors. You buy it because of what the benefit of four doors means to you. If you have a big family, you know how difficult a two-door car can be.

The seasoned salesperson not only talks about features, but more importantly, what those features mean to the customer. The process is known as "benefit selling." A benefit is the value the feature has to the customer. To do this effectively you must make it clear to a customer the value link that exists between the feature and benefit.

Features & Benefits. The backbone of every effective presentation is features and benefits. They are the salesperson's means of concisely explaining the value of the product or service to the customer. While the novice salesperson tends to sell feature after feature, the professional salesperson focuses on what those features will do for the customer and sells benefits. By definition:

A *feature* is a characteristic of a product or service.

A *benefit* is the value of the feature to the customer.

Benefits focus on both the hidden and obvious value that is important to the customer. It is this value that will ultimately sell the customer. It is to your competitive advantage to sell on benefits rather than features. Benefits answer the customer's question, *"What does that mean for me or my company?"* Benefits are easily generated by simply identifying a characteristic (feature) of the product or service and asking yourself, *"So what? What does that mean to the customer?"*

Tactical Benefits. In today's competitive market, salespeople must go beyond the standard feature-benefit presentation. Tactical benefits further customize the value of your particular product or service to the customer. Assuming your price is the

LICENSE TO SELL

same or more than the competition's, you must build added value into your product or service. This means not only convincing the customer that your product or service is better, but also that it is worth the extra money.

Tactical benefits appeal to the decision maker's goals and objectives. Positioning benefits of your product or service into the corporate and personal strategies of the company and decision maker creates a strong customer relationship.

Tactical benefits are categorized in three major areas:

- ✔ dollars
- ✔ productivity
- ✔ status

Dollars. Dollars pertain to money. A prospective customer who is dollar-conscious will be motivated by dollar-oriented benefits. You would tailor your benefits to focus on the low cost, savings, and overall dollar or "bottom line" gains that can be achieved by using your product or service.

Productivity. Productivity focuses on performance-related issues. A prospective customer who is interested in productivity gains will be motivated by enhanced performance-type benefits. You would tailor your benefits to focus on time savings, ease of use and overall production gains that can be achieved by using your product or service.

Status. Status focuses on the image a prospective customer wants to project to internal or external customers. You would tailor your benefits to focus on image, status and the perception of others with the use of your product or service.

Example
Product: Styrofoam Cup
Feature: Styrofoam
Dollar: low cost per unit, disposable, lower shipping cost
Productivity: disposable, no need to wash, various sizes
Status: promotes cost-saving image of company

During the Sale   **SALES SKILLS**

Your Mission

Identify a prospective customer and a feature that would be of interest. Then identify one, two or all three tactical benefits that relate to the same feature.

Customer: _____

Feature: _____

Dollar Benefit: _____
_____

Productivity Benefit: _____
_____

Status Benefit: _____
_____

Feature: _____

Dollar Benefit: _____
_____

Productivity Benefit: _____
_____

Status Benefit: _____
_____

Feature: _____

Dollar Benefit: _____
_____

Productivity Benefit: _____
_____

Status Benefit: _____
_____

LICENSE TO SELL

Positioning Yourself as a Benefit. If your company's products or services already have unique benefits, you're already at an advantage. If you don't have any unique product or service benefits, sell yourself. Here are some ways you can position yourself as a benefit to your customers:

✔ company product knowledge expert

✔ competitor product knowledge expert

✔ expert professional selling skills

✔ consultative selling approach

✔ problem solver

✔ reliable

✔ expert customer service

✔ personal customer service

✔ visionary

✔ ability to tap business contacts in the industry

✔ integrity; ability to walk away from customers you can't genuinely help

✔ offer your experience on possible use and implementation of your product or service

✔ offer your home telephone number

✔ start your own newsletter

The more you can do to obtain and keep customers, the better your chances for sales success. Remember, your competition may be doing the same. The professional is always looking for ways to improve himself or herself.

Transitions. Transitioning from a feature to a benefit is important, and the words you use must be intentional and direct. Here are some transition statements and words you can use to bridge from features to benefits.

✔ *Our product has...*(feature)

✔ *And what this means to you is...*(benefit)

During the Sale **SALES SKILLS**

- ✔ *And how this applies to your specific need is...*(benefit)
- ✔ *And this will solve your problem by...*(benefit)

Your Mission

Complete the transition statements by customizing them to your product or service.

Our product has...
_____
_____
_____

And what this means to you is...
_____
_____
_____

And how this applies to your specific need is...
_____
_____
_____

And this will solve your problem by...
_____
_____
_____

LICENSE TO SELL

During the Sale **SALES SKILLS**

Adding Value to What You Sell

You can sell anything to anybody and get your asking price. In sales, you can have your cake and eat it too — if you add value to what you sell.

One of the most powerful ways that a salesperson can add value to her product or service is by taking advantage of the opportunity to make a presentation. An effective presentation can help prospective customers see beyond what's on the outside to what's on the inside — the hidden benefits — as the real value to the customer.

It's important to understand the customer's decision making process. The sale is often made when the customer realizes it will cost more to do *nothing* about their current situation or problem, than to do *something* about it. When customers have no doubt that what they are buying has great value associated with it, not only will they buy it, they will buy more! It is up to you as to how much value you add into your sales presentation.

Quantify Savings. It comes down to dollars and sense. If you sell a service for $100 and deliver only a $50 or $80 presentation, it's no wonder the customer is skeptical or indifferent to you or your service. Why would he buy something when he sees no value in it? One clue that you may not be adding enough value to your presentation is frequently encountering the customer who stalls by asking for information or literature. Think about it, what she is saying is, *"Your presentation didn't convince me that I should make this decision today so maybe your literature might tell me something you forgot or overlooked."*

It is in your best interest to quantify all savings that can be achieved with your product or service. Not just with one use but a lifetime of uses. For instance:

✔ How long will it take to pay for itself?

✔ How much time and effort will it save the customer?

143

LICENSE TO SELL

✔ What could or would the customer do with those extra dollars?

Once you get the prospective customer to see the opportunity your product or service represents, he will not want to let this opportunity walk out the door!

Your Mission

List three ways to quantify your product or service.

1. _____
_____
_____
_____

2. _____
_____
_____
_____

3. _____
_____
_____
_____

During the Sale **SALES SKILLS**

Selling Against the Competition

In order to get prospective customers to buy from you, it is key to know what choices your customers have. Your goal is to learn what your competition does well, then fully develop your own strengths to give the customer a choice. If customers do not see a difference between your strengths and your competitors, then they may be forced to choose based solely on price and availability.

Begin by thinking about the "unique strengths" of your product or service. You start here because this is where the customer starts to think. The customer will have a concept of your "unique strengths" and that allows you to relate your product or service to that concept. By definition, unique strengths are the distinguishable differences that you can communicate between your product or service and your competition.

Two important questions that you need to answer are:

✔ *What does the prospective customer really need?*

✔ *How can I uniquely deliver it?*

You are looking for a fit! Keep in mind that your strengths alone are not enough for customers to choose you. You've got to be able to communicate information about your strengths that make you stand out from the others.

This is even more critical in a very competitive marketplace, particularly if the competitors do not have distinguishable differences! In a highly competitive marketplace, unless you sell "unique strengths," the customer is forced to do the sorting and — nine times out of ten — they'll choose on the basis of price and availability alone. This approach minimizes the importance of price competition and allows you to do "value added" selling.

Identifying Unique Strengths. Here are some types of unique strengths:

✔ PEOPLE — the associates and/or employees that truly stand out in the opinions of customers.

LICENSE TO SELL

✔ PRODUCT — the physical features that are distinguishable.

✔ SERVICE — the various levels of service offered.

✔ TRAINING — quality and amount of training your associates and managers receive, i.e., new-hire orientation, on-going training, etc.

✔ EXPERIENCE/TRACK RECORD — length of time you have been in business.

✔ COMPANY NAME — the value of your brand name, Recognition Programs, etc.

✔ CUSTOMER BASE — the types of customers who currently do business with you that can be leveraged.

✔ REPUTATION — the image your product or service has in the marketplace.

✔ LOCATION — advantages of your location over a competitor.

✔ GUARANTEE — the power of your guarantee of service.

✔ YOU — the selling skills you possess, your dedication to the company and any unique qualifications and experiences.

Your Mission

Here's how you can identify the unique strengths of your product or service.

List one of your top competitors:

_____

During the Sale **SALES SKILLS**

Place a check mark and list all of your unique strengths that apply when compared to your top competitor. Write in any that are not listed on the "Other" line.

People ❑ *We're Stronger* ❑ *They're Stronger*
_____
_____

Product ❑ *We're Stronger* ❑ *They're Stronger*
_____
_____

Service ❑ *We're Stronger* ❑ *They're Stronger*
_____
_____

Training ❑ *We're Stronger* ❑ *They're Stronger*
_____
_____

Experience/Track Record ❑ *We're Stronger* ❑ *They're Stronger*
_____
_____

LICENSE TO SELL

Company Name ❑ *We're Stronger* ❑ *They're Stronger*
_____

_____

Customer Base ❑ *We're Stronger* ❑ *They're Stronger*
_____

_____

Reputation ❑ *We're Stronger* ❑ *They're Stronger*
_____

_____

Location ❑ *We're Stronger* ❑ *They're Stronger*
_____

_____

Guarantee ❑ *We're Stronger* ❑ *They're Stronger*
_____

_____

You ❑ *We're Stronger* ❑ *They're Stronger*
_____

_____

Other ❑ *We're Stronger* ❑ *They're Stronger*
_____

_____

Do this exercise for each of your competitors.

During the Sale · SALES SKILLS

As you look back over all the possible unique strengths, you will *not* have a strength advantage for each category. But try to come up with several areas of differentiation from each competitor. Avoid listing strengths that are no different from your competitor. Instead, focus on capabilities which are "unique" or better.

It is time for the final tests — prove it! With this list of truly unique strengths, you should be able to write a brief sentence for each unique strength proving its value to the customer. Your answers should be brief. Simply say why you are different from the competition. Choose a strength and write out:

We are the <u>only</u> ones who . . .

_____
_____
_____
_____

Choose a different strength and write out:

We are <u>*different*</u> because . . .

_____
_____
_____
_____

Remember, you can prove your validity by giving references from satisfied customers or by a money-back guarantee. Realize these strengths will change for each individual customer because needs change for every person. It's important to realize that sometimes we are not unique. A competitor may get the sale because they happened to be the strongest or offer a unique benefit. Often, it is easier for a company *not to change* vendors just for the sake of change.

LICENSE TO SELL

Track Your Competitors. Competition is everywhere! Depending on your industry, it may be difficult for just one person to keep up with all the forms of competition. If possible, make this a shared responsibility among employees. Assign people to monitor key competitors or outsource the responsibility to a service provider that tracks your business. Here are some ways you can take an objective look at your competition:

- ✔ Get on your competition's mailing list, if they have one.
- ✔ Visit their web site regularly.
- ✔ Have friends or business associates visit your competition and give a perspective on their goods and services.
- ✔ Advertising agencies and Public Relations firms often provide a "clipping service" that will pull articles on companies or industries you want tracked, including your own organization.
- ✔ If you don't know who your competition is, then ask your customers!

Your first step is to analyze who you have lost business to over the past 3-6 months. Then, go out and learn all about them. You need to become as knowledgeable about their strengths and weaknesses as you are about your own. Make this competitive analysis an annual budgeting exercise. It is vital to keep a constant eye on your existing and new competitors.

During the Sale — SALES SKILLS

Buying Signals

Smart salespeople know how to read a prospect's body language, as well as what the customer says, to know the right time to close the sale. Signals can come in different forms. If you're face-to-face with a prospective customer, you can watch her eyes, facial expressions, arms, shoulders, or listen to her words. If on the phone, you must rely on your listening skills and zero in on her tone of voice and words. There are two types of buying signs: verbal and nonverbal.

Verbal Buying Signals. Any words, phrases or utterances that signify in some way that the prospective customer desires to possess your product or service are buying signals.

Positive signals include:

- ✔ I'm sold!
- ✔ Where do I sign?
- ✔ Great!
- ✔ Sounds good.
- ✔ We are getting there.
- ✔ When can I get it delivered?
- ✔ Looks good!
- ✔ No more questions.
- ✔ Will you take a check?
- ✔ Do you accept American Express?
- ✔ Do I get a discount if I pay cash?
- ✔ Let's shake on it.
- ✔ OK!
- ✔ What is your return policy?
- ✔ Can I get it in blue?
- ✔ What is the price including tax?

LICENSE TO SELL

Negative signals include:

✔ Wait a minute here.

✔ Can't do it.

✔ That is not acceptable.

NonVerbal. Prospective customers also communicate without saying a word. Nonverbal buying signals can be positive or negative.

Positive signals include:

✔ Sparkle in the eyes

✔ Friendliness

✔ Relaxed gestures and posture

✔ Laughter

✔ Big smiles

✔ Head nodding in agreement — North/South direction!

✔ Arms open

✔ Good eye contact

Negative signals include:

✔ Anger

✔ Frowns

✔ Head nodding - East/West Direction!

✔ Arms folded

✔ Little eye contact

During the Sale **SALES SKILLS**

Your Mission

For you, which is tougher to identify: verbal or nonverbal buying signals?

How can you improve identifying buying signals?

Face-to-face:

Over the phone:

LICENSE TO SELL

During the Sale   **SALES SKILLS**

Psychology & Traits of the Super Salesperson

What ingredients make up an effective and successful salesperson? No one can say for sure, but there are some characteristics and traits that successful salespeople tend to exude more so than those who are ineffective. The successful salesperson in the 21st century must be:

- sharp, honed and polished
- prepared for change
- a good listener
- excellent interpersonal skills
- possess total product knowledge
- empathetic to the customer's needs
- positive in attitude
- ready for any objection
- familiar with the competition
- willing and able to adapt her presentation on the fly and shift gears at a moment's notice
- lean and mean, but at the same time be the customer's best friend
- always smiling
- upbeat
- a superman
- a politician
- ethical
- consultative
- unafraid of no, but welcome no as an opportunity

LICENSE TO SELL

Every successful salesperson we know fits this mold. While today it is the exception, tomorrow it will be the expectation.

Consultative. Good salespeople are consultative. They ask questions and never assume that what they have to sell will satisfy your needs 100%, at least in the beginning.

Interpersonal Skills. Good salespeople know how to listen and ask open-ended and close-ended questions. They also are able to facilitate discussions and remain neutral even in heated selling situations.

Positive Attitude. Another ingredient that makes up a good salesperson is attitude. We have found that most salespeople who are around for the long-term tend to be positive people. They have an optimistic view of life and are usually upbeat, cheerful, smiling, and possess above average interpersonal skills.

A positive attitude is important for a few reasons. Perhaps the most important is to counteract the customer's neutral or often negative outlook on life. Another reason positive attitude is important gets to the heart of selling — and that is the amount of rejection, both personal and professional, the average salesperson must accept to be successful.

It's realistic to say that eight out of ten prospective customers will say no. When only two customers agree to buy from you, you are a successful salesperson. Why? Because two out of ten (or a 20% close ratio) is true success. It takes a positive mental attitude to get through those eight *nos* to get to the two *yeses*.

Five, ten or eighty rejections may be too much for novice salespeople to tolerate, and as a result their attitude becomes contaminated with negativity. At this point, due to this self-imposed barrier, the salesperson with his negative view of life, his product, his company, and his customers, is defeated even before the selling process begins.

Keeping your attitude positive is a not just a selling skill, but a philosophy — a way of doing business. It is something you must be aware of at all times during the day and for the rest of your sales career. You must always look at the bright side and never or rarely let your negative attitude get the best of you.

During the Sale **SALES SKILLS**

Your Mission

Survey/interview a few of your good customers. Ask some of the following questions:

Why do/did they buy from you?

_____
_____
_____
_____

What personal characteristics about you do they like best?

_____
_____
_____
_____

How are you different from other salespeople the customer deals with?

_____
_____
_____
_____

One a scale of 1 to 10, with 10 being the highest, how would you rate your positive attitude?

_____
_____
_____
_____

LICENSE TO SELL

During the Sale   **SALES SKILLS**

The Art of Closing

Very simply, the *"close"* is what selling is all about. Like the final curtain at the end of a play, the presentation of a check at the conclusion of a meal, and of course the close in a sales presentation, it is the time when the customer is asked to do something — make some kind of a decision. For many, closing is easier said than done. Why? Because many salespeople don't know when to close or are afraid. They are afraid the prospective customer might say no. Successful salespeople operate on a different mindset when it comes to the closing process because they make closing a part of their overall selling strategy.

Closers Wanted. Closing is a critical skill for a salesperson to master. Do it well and you will have a long, rewarding and profitable career as a salesperson. If you don't do it well, sales will forever be a struggle. In sales, unlike a lot of other professions, you can't hide behind your contacts, your degree, or your general experience. In sales, your ability as a salesperson is quantified in the form of results. You get measured. How many sales did you make? How much revenue did you bring in? How many new customers did you generate?

For the most part, your boss doesn't really care how many literature packs you mailed, how many people you shook hands with, or how many presentations you made. Bottom line: how many customers did you close? How much new business did you create? That's what counts!

Remember to Close. In order to remember to close, make it part of your overall selling strategy. You can do this by trying to close early and often on *little things*. Why? Because most customers do not like to make big decisions at the end of the selling process. Ideally, you gain closure on little things during the selling process. Think of them as minor agreements that get the customer's head moving North and South throughout the call. Think of the ultimate YES as a sum of smaller *yeses*!

LICENSE TO SELL

If you are selling a watch that automatically changes time when the seasons do, you might say:

✔ *Isn't that a nice color?*

✔ *Can you see yourself using this?*

✔ *Wouldn't it be nice to never to change time again?*

✔ *Would you like to try it on?*

✔ *Can I wrap it for you?*

If the prospect agrees, the salesperson no longer has to sell the concept of buying a watch that changes time when the seasons do. The customer can focus on the color and ease of use. By deciding at the end only if they want it wrapped up it makes the decision easier because the customer has been making decisions on *little things* along the way.

Your Mission

In your sales job, make a list of *little things* you can close on in the selling process:

_____

_____

_____

_____

_____

_____

_____

_____

Can you see how making the closing process part of your overall selling strategy will keep you from forgetting to close?

The Fear of No. The other significant reason for not closing is the fear of hearing the customer say *"no."* It is easy to overcome this fear if you have built rapport and trust throughout the selling process. Prospective customers will be more inclined to buy from someone who has shown a genuine interest in them throughout the selling process. Remember, the reason for rapport building is that it makes it harder for customers to say *"no"* to someone they know or like.

When a customer objects to something, he is doing you a favor by giving you a reason for not buying. Sometimes the reason is vague — such as just "No." Don't assume it means *"Not now, I'm not ready to buy yet."* As a sales pro it is your job to find out what has not been covered that is keeping the customer from saying *"yes."*

You might respond to vague statements by using one or all of these strategies:

- ✔ Silence — Sometimes a customer will elaborate without any additional prompting.
- ✔ *Oh?* — This subtle one word query may be just enough to nudge the customer to expand on his no.
- ✔ *Why do you say no?*

Treat the reason for the customer not buying the same way you would an opportunity. Use a closed probe to confirm the need then (re)introduce features and benefits.

You might say something like:

"So the reason you didn't want to move forward with the purchase is due to the price. Is that correct?"

"What you're looking for is a lower price, right?"

"If the price was reduced by 5%, would you make the purchase?"

LICENSE TO SELL

Your Mission

Think about great spots that make customers feel comfortable to agree to do business with you? Time-sharing businesses actually have closing rooms.

Now list the locations that you like to use to close on customers:

_____
_____
_____
_____
_____
_____
_____
_____

Are there other locations where you should be doing more closings? List them:

_____
_____
_____
_____
_____
_____
_____
_____

Closing in the Sales Process. Why do you close? To move the sales process forward and ultimately accomplish the purpose of your call or presentation. Traditionally, it may be to get the customer's commitment to buy or place an order.

However, depending on the complexity and nature of the product and service you sell, your close may be:

✔ to gain another appointment;

✔ to gain an introduction to someone else in the company;

✔ to obtain permission to submit a proposal;

✔ to obtain a signature on a contract.

Depending on the type of product or service you sell, each stage of the selling cycle has a purpose and a sales objective. Refer to the exercise you completed on page 128.

Transitioning into a Close. An effective close should be a natural extension of the selling process. Not some contrived line that appears out of left field. With that in mind, lets look at different styles of closing.

A good transition line for closing is:

"Does this proposal meet with your needs?"

If so, then pick your style of close.

Closing Lines. Your close can be "direct" which assumes the sale and directly asks the customer to take action or "indirect" which prompts an open-ended response that identifies an action. Here are some closing lines you may want to try.

Direct Closes

✔ *Will that be cash or credit card?*

✔ *Do you want delivery during the morning or afternoon?*

✔ *Shall I wrap it up for you?*

✔ *Are you willing to give us your business?*

✔ *Do you have a preference between the red or the blue?*

LICENSE TO SELL

- ✔ *How soon can we start?*
- ✔ *Will you sign the purchase order today?*
- ✔ *Can I stop by tomorrow and pick up the signed contract?*
- ✔ *How would you like to set up the billing and deposit arrangements?*
- ✔ *Can we do business?*

Indirect Closes

- ✔ *Are there any other questions I can answer?*
- ✔ *How else can I help you make a buying decision?*
- ✔ *Is there anything else you would like to see?*
- ✔ *Are you in the market for...?*
- ✔ *What is the next step in your mind?*
- ✔ *Is there anyone else involved in making the purchase decision?*
- ✔ *On a scale of 1 to 10, how close are we to doing business together?*
- ✔ *Is there a date in which you have to have a purchase decision made by?*

Your Mission

Add a few of your own closing lines:

_____
_____
_____
_____

During the Sale   **SALES SKILLS**

Different Types of Closes

There are a variety of techniques and methods that are used to get a customer to move to the next step. Given the fact that many new salespeople lack closing skills, possessing this information will allow you to pick a style or strategy that you feel comfortable with and that fits the customer's situation. One close does not fit all. The more closes you have in your professional sales skill bag, the more sales you will make.

While some closes will become your favorites that you use everyday, others will be used every now and then depending on the customer or the situation. The point is that a professional salesperson possess the skills to get the job done — to close — to make the sale.

The Trial Close

This is often called the close within a close. A trial close is simply a question that you ask the customer that assumes ownership of your product or service. Such as:

"Which color model of our product would you and your staff prefer, red or blue?"

"When service begins, would you like to start that day or wait until the end of the month?"

These are questions you ask at the beginning, middle and end of the sales call. If the customer answers you, it is as if he already has assumed ownership of your product or service. This is an important psychological aspect of the sale because it answers the question, *"Is the customer going to buy?"* By asking questions and obtaining customer answers that assume customer ownership or use of the product or service, it becomes easier for the customer to say yes.

Tom Hopkins uses the term *"minor tie-downs"* to describe a method of trial closing that should be in every salesperson's skill arsenal. Minor tie-downs are another way to continually get the customer to agree with you or the benefits associated with your product or service.

LICENSE TO SELL

Use tie downs anywhere in the call: the beginning of a sentence, the middle, or attach them to the end. Such as:

✔ *Aren't they?*

✔ *Aren't you?*

✔ *Can't you?*

✔ *Don't you?*

✔ *Shouldn't it?*

✔ *Wouldn't you?*

✔ *Isn't it?*

✔ *Didn't it?*

✔ *Won't they?*

✔ *Wasn't it?*

✔ *Hasn't she?*

✔ *Doesn't it?*

✔ *Couldn't it?*

When speaking to the customer, it would sound something like this:

"Wouldn't it be nice to solve that problem once and for all Mr. Customer? Don't you agree that a change is going to save you lots of time and money? And saving that time and money is important to you, isn't it? And you could invest that money in other parts of the firm or just pocket it as additional profit, couldn't you?"

Imagine for a moment you were the customer in the above scenario. Did you find yourself agreeing with every question posed? You did, didn't you? See you just did it again! It is an easy way to continually gain customer agreement, isn't it? See you just did it again! The strategy here is to get the customer saying *"yes"* and nodding his head in agreement throughout the sales call.

Assume the Sale Close

In the Assume the Sale Close, you really do this right from the start. You do not ask if and when the customer will purchase. You just assume the purchase will be made. Questions include:

"When do you want delivery?"

"Where would you like the delivery people to put it once it arrives?"

"Do you want the green model or the brown one?"

Urgency Close

The Urgency Close stresses the timeliness of the customer's decision. Statements and questions that stress urgency include:

"Order by midnight tonight while supplies last!"

"First come, first served."

"Order before the price changes go into effect on Monday."

"A signature today would guarantee delivery on Wednesday; a signature at a later time will not."

Tell a Story Close

Tell the customer about a similar customer who bought the product and is now using it. Tell them how the order was placed, the deposits and signatures gained, and how the product was delivered. Then just finish by saying, *"Would you like to do the same?"*

Take Away Close

The Take Away Close is based on the fear of losing or presenting a challenge. The people who tend to buy-in to this type of close are decisive go-getters who know what they want and just do it. To address the fear of losing, you might say:

LICENSE TO SELL

"It's possible, I'll have to check and make sure that this item hasn't already been sold to someone who came in last night."

"I don't think we have any more in the color you like in the store and we don't expect another in for two months."

To present a challenge, you might say:

"I don't think this is for you."

"I don't think you're ready for an upgrade."

"I'm not sure this car is for you."

Action Close

The Action Close is designed to get the customer to do something positive. For example, you could:

Hand the customer the pen and put the agreement in front of him.

Hold the car keys in your hand and say, *"The decision is yours."*

Pick up the phone and ask the customer to get his boss in the room for final approval or his secretary to draw up the necessary paperwork.

Hold out your hand ready for a handshake and ask, *"Do we have a deal?"*

Alternative Choice Close

This close is all about choice — presenting options to the customer and allowing her to choose. You might say:

"Do you want it in green or blue?"

"Is Friday or Tuesday better for our first appointment?"

"Did you want the upgrade or the standard model?"

During the Sale   **SALES SKILLS**

If the customer responds to one of the alternatives you provide, the sale is made. A rule of thumb here is that the customer will usually pick the smaller or less expensive of the two alternatives you present. If you want to make a $10 sale, don't say do you want the $5 or the $10 model. You should say do you want the $10 or the $15 model.

Summary Close

The summary close is one of the oldest and one of the most professional closes you can use. Simply review the benefits the customer has accepted during the presentation and ask for the sale or action step. This approach is effective for a couple reasons. First, it reminds the customer of what he or she liked about your product or service just prior to asking for the sale or action step. Second, it allows you to get a *"yes"* or agreement for each benefit making the ultimate yes easier to obtain. Such as:

"So you agree that our service is 20% faster than your current service, which in turn will allow you to serve your customers even more effectively, correct?"

At this point you should literally stop and wait for the customer to say *"yes"* or give you a nonverbal agreement of some kind. Not doing so is shortchanging your sales presentation and reducing your ability to close effectively.

You then proceed with the next benefit:

"And you also agree that our service has the back-end office support and experience you need to quickly and effectively solve any problems should one ever occur, right?

Wait for the customer to say yes. Let me also say, that the yes is important but this approach also allows for a *"no"* to pop up. It is for this reason a lot of inexperienced salespeople don't like it for fear of getting *"no"* for an answer. The *"no"* is a good thing — it allows you to effectively pinpoint the portion of your presentation that was not as convincing as you thought, or for some reason has caused the customer to have second thoughts. Should a *"no"* occur, simply probe to ensure understanding of

LICENSE TO SELL

the concern and offer appropriate features and benefits necessary to support your claims. Remember at this time, you may want to use as much supporting evidence as possible to leave no doubt in the customer's mind.

Finally, after gaining agreement on each individual benefit — not feature — you are ready to ask for the sale or ask the customer to take action. This close is one that should almost always be followed by another. The Summary Close could follow the Direct Close or the Suggestion Close.

Suggestion Close

The suggestion close is non-threatening and keeps the salesperson and selling environment relatively neutral. When the time comes, simply begin by saying:

"Mr. Customer, based on what we discussed today, and more importantly your specific needs, we suggest that you select the x43 unit. The x43 will meet your output need of 50 units per minute. If you recall, the x43 will produce 55 to 65 units per minute depending on how you load it. And, it will also be meeting your cost need of a monthly payment below $500 per month. We recommend, like many of our customers have, you select the 36 month payment plan. This will provide you with a monthly payment of just $478. And finally, we suggest to ensure the best payback on your investment, that you have the unit installed and running by August 1. Fair enough?"

"What I suggest is...."

"What I would recommend is..."

"The next step is..."

"Based on my experience, I would recommend..."

This is a very professional and cordial way to ask for the order but not appear too aggressive to the customer.

Question with a Question Close

If a customer asks, *"Can you deliver it here by Tuesday?"* Your response might be, *"If we could guarantee delivery here by Tuesday, do we have a deal?"* In other words, you make the question the pivot in the sale and turn it around as the close. The customer would rarely ask a question if he or she was not genuinely interested in finding out the answer, so this kind of close works well towards the very end of a sale, even more so when a few previous objections have already arisen.

Trial Balloon Close

The trial balloon close is a good one because it allows you to test your close without any real commitment on your part or the part of the customer. Like it sounds, you make a suggestion or offer or direct close in the form of a trial balloon. If it floats you have a winner. If the balloon gets shot down by the customer, that's OK because it was only a trial balloon and not the real thing.

Trial balloons usually lead with the words *"What if"* such as:

"What if we were to lower the price by 5% as an inducement to gain your commitment today? Would we earn your business?"

"What if there was a way to get the price you want and at the same time allow us to meet our minimum pricing requirement? How would that sound?"

Ideally, what you are looking for is the customer to say something like, *"I'd sign up today," "I'd do the deal"* or *"When can we start?"* With that kind of reaction, you simply respond:

"Great, to make it happen sign here."

"Just give me the OK and I'll make it happen."

LICENSE TO SELL

Ben Franklin/T Close

The Ben Franklin close is as old as Ben Franklin and a little hokey, but we've included it to present an array of closes. The close comes with its own story and it goes something like this. Ben Franklin, one of the fathers of our country, made thousands of complex and important decisions over his lifetime. Many of those decisions have proven to be the right ones hundreds of years later. How did he do it? What Ben would do is draw a big T on a piece of paper. On the right hand side of the T he would write down all the positives associated with the decision. On the left side of the T he would write down all the minuses. Then he would complete each side of the T filling in the +'s and -'s. The side that had the most items was the winner and the decision would be made.

Here's how you would do it. Review the +s such as:

"You stated that you liked the fact that our prices better than any you have seen, right?"

Turn the pad towards the customer and hand him the pen. Then say:

"Write down the words Better Price under the +. What else do you like about it Mr. Customer?"

During the Sale   SALES SKILLS

Allow the customer to come up with as many as he can. Hint at benefits he accepted during the call and have him write each one down. When he can't remember any more by himself, assist him by adding any additional benefits he may have forgotten to mention. The list should be about 10 items long.

Once you run out of positives, the next step is to move over to the negatives such as:

"Now Mr. Customer I want you to list any negatives you have about the product."

Do not participate in this part of the close. At this point it is 100 percent customer. If you offer negatives, you're working against yourself.

Usually, the customer will only be able to find 2 or 3 negatives. When he is done, you say something like:

"If Ben Franklin was to make another one of his wise decisions, it's obvious he would go with our product. Do you agree with Ben on this one?"

Wait for the customer to say *"yes"* and then say, *"It is a wise decision."*

Customer Sells Himself Close

This is a simple little close that again works well when coupled with other closes. At the end of the call simply ask the customer to summarize what she likes best about the product. Get the customer to state as many features and benefits as possible. After doing so say something like:

"You sold me! When would you like to start?"

Try it/Puppy Dog Close

The Puppy Dog Close has been around as long as puppy dogs. Imagine if you went to the pet store and found a cute little lovable bundle of fur — a puppy dog that just made you smile from ear to ear. He loved you as much as you loved him. But, you don't know if you want the dog or not. The pet shop owner

173

LICENSE TO SELL

then makes it easy for you and says, *"Go ahead take him home to the kids and see if they like him. If they don't you can always bring him back in the morning."* By allowing the customer to try it, take it home and use it, and worse yet let the kids fall in love with it, the puppy is as good as sold.

If your product or service lends itself to being borrowed or used for a period of time with the option of the customer returning it, this close may work for you. By removing the decision until after the customer has possession — thereby using and benefiting from the product — it sells itself.

Let Me Ask My Manager Close

This is the classic new car salesman close. You negotiate and talk, and talk and talk some more. Finally, the salesperson says, *"I don't know if I could get you the car for that price, let me go ask my manager."* Prior to leaving, the salesperson would be sure to isolate the objection and try to obtain some form of conditional commitment from you. He might say something like, *"Before I go ask him he is going to want to know, if we give you the car at that price, will you purchase it today?"*

Assuming you say yes the salesperson then disappears around the corner. What does the salesperson do while he is away? If you only knew — having a cigarette, a soda or a cup of coffee. Sometimes he even talks to his manager. Assuming the price is OK, he returns and says, *"Good news! You're the owner of a new car."*

If he returns with his manager you have been what is called in the sales world TO'd or *Turned Over*. Usually the turn over will require the salesperson introducing the manager to the customer and stating the situation that exists:

"Our customer, Mr. Smith wants the car and really likes the way it drives, however the only way he would take the car off the lot today is if we could let it go for $18,500. I told him that it's way below list and that it would be your decision as to whether or not we could even consider such an offer"

During the Sale **SALES SKILLS**

If the salesperson really wants to use some sales psychology, when he returns he sits on the same side of the table as the customer and lets his manager take his seat. This puts the salesperson on the customer's team. Now it's customer and the salesperson versus the manager. You will be surprised how often the customer will turn to the salesperson for advice. Also, in the event the deal blows up, the sales manager becomes the bad guy and the salesperson may still have a chance to salvage the sale. It's effective and works — just ask any car salesperson.

The COLUMBO —Just One More Thing Close

This close is used when all else fails. Literally, when you are packing up or walking out the door, you turn to the customer and ask:

"Just for the record and so I don't make the same mistake again, what could I have done or said differently that would have made you buy?"

"One more thing, what could I have done or said to get your business?"

At this stage in the call the customer's guard is down. The customer might just give you the opening you need and tell you what you missed. With that information you may be able to jump right in, offer the missing piece of information and make the sale.

The Silent Close

After asking for the business, give the gift of silence. Let the prospective customer respond first to your close. Give him an opportunity to say *"yes!"* Remember, the first one who speaks loses! If you get a no answer, don't take it personally. It may mean, no — not just yet. There may be other issues to resolve. You could say something such as:

"You may be thinking what is the best way to get started. Let me show you how another customer did it. Can I have your okay to proceed?"

LICENSE TO SELL

In other words, if you must speak — keep it focused on the close and ask for the business again!

Your Mission

Write the close that you use most often.

_____
_____
_____
_____
_____

Look back through the chapter and write at least two new closes you would be comfortable with trying on a customer.

1. _____
_____
_____
_____
_____
_____

2. _____
_____
_____
_____
_____
_____

After the Sale   **SALES SKILLS**

How to Turn Objections into Opportunities

It is often said that the sale begins when the customer says *"no."* Up until that point you are merely a presenter or marketer of information. Getting the customer to move from *"no"* to *"yes"* is the skill of selling.

Objections are part of the selling process you must learn to love. An objection occurs when a customer has serious doubts or questions about your product or service prior to purchase. How effectively you handle your customers' objections will determine the outcome of your sales efforts.

The novice salesperson often looks down on objections and does his best to minimize or downplay them. He does this by telling the customer his concern is unwarranted, tries to change the subject, or answers a simple yes or no question with long and drawn-out explanations.

The successful salesperson welcomes the objection and treats it with respect that it deserves. If it is important for the customer to take time to ask the question, or express his concern over a feature or lack thereof, it is important for the salesperson to ensure the customer gets the exact answer he or she is looking for — even if it means losing the sale.

How to Handle Objections. Here is a step-by-step approach to effectively handle objections:

1) The first step is to make sure you understand the objection. Take a moment to clarify any vague customer comments such as *"It is a matter of timing."*

2) Never assume that you can read the customer's mind. The last thing you want to do is to assume understanding only to find out the customer is talking about something else.

3) Once you clarify and confirm the objection or think you have a complete understanding of it, you should then take the time to confirm it. While it may seem that this step is

LICENSE TO SELL

redundant, the strategy here is to get the customer to define exactly what the problem is so you can apply a customized solution. An example such as:

"So what you're saying Mr. Customer is...(restate the objection), is that right?"

The key here is to get the customer to agree with your understanding of the concern. More importantly, if the customer says *"No, that's not it"* you have an opportunity to again clarify exactly what the concern or question is.

If the customer's objection is in the form of a question, simply answer it with a question:

"Does it copy more than 50 pages a minute?"

Your response, *"Would you like it to copy more than 50 pages a minute?"*

In the above example, we know the product can copy faster than 50 pages a minute. But what if it couldn't? You should try to massage the objection into something you can handle through the use of a clarifying or confirming question. Such as:

"Does it copy 50 pages a minute?"

Your response, *"It sounds to me that it is important that you get your jobs done fast and on time, is that true?"*

Most likely the customer will agree to a statement like that. Clarifying questions are important because they show you were listening, and more importantly, that you are moving in the same direction as the customer.

If the objection is not based on a simple question, you should then probe to uncover any additional hidden objections. Do not fall into the trap of answering the objection only to have another and another arise. Handling objections this way is like trying to hold a big wet slippery fish with your bare hands; you may be able to do it, but it is not pretty and the chances of slipping away from you are great.

4) After you confirm and understand the objection, acknowledge it and probe for more concerns. You might say:

"I can understand your concern with (briefly state the customer's objection). It sounds like that is an important issue and one that I would like to address. In the best interest of time, before I respond, is there any other reason you feel our product wouldn't meet your needs?"

Wait for a response. If you get one, probe it. Understand it. Confirm it. Acknowledge it. And then, ask for another. Continue to do this until the customer has no more objections. After she says no, ask her one more time just to make sure. You will be surprised how many objections pop out just because you ask twice.

5) Finally, you may want to ask the following question as a way to test the buyer's true interest or to close the sale:

"So if we can effectively meet and exceed all of your concerns, do we have a deal?"

Think of this process as getting all your ducks in a row. This approach of asking for and tabling all objections allows you to reorder the objections to best suit your needs and ultimately make the strongest case for your product or service. You may want to put the hardest one last, or maybe first. You may find that you can combine two into one and handle them together. Bottom line: Getting objections out in the open allows you to plan and mentally prepare if even only for a minute or two.

If the objection is based on a feature or benefit that your product doesn't possess, say so. It's often best to be frank and up front with a customer. If your customer feels at anytime that you are being evasive, you will lose trust for the entire call and probably the entire relationship. At the same time, if you answer honestly and state your reasons in a professional manner, you build customer trust. This is very important for anyone who sells a product or service that involves repeat sales, works in a fixed sales territory, or must visit the same prospects over time to make a sale.

LICENSE TO SELL

The product you offer today may not work, but the one you offer tomorrow may. Conversely, the customer's need for your product or service may not exist today, but it may tomorrow. If you have built a relationship based on honesty and trust, your chances of future success are far greater.

Requests for Info. Often the customer asks questions or raises objections that simply requires you to provide more information even after you have provided her with a complete and detailed presentation. The key is to have a couple sources available to handle the more information request. Newspaper and magazine articles, testimonials or a copy of your guarantee or warranty are credible and convincing sources of information. Simply hand the printed document to the customer and let it speak for itself. If it is a long article or large document, pre-highlight or underline the key points you want the reader to evaluate. Also, be able to circle or highlight key points on the spot.

Sometimes the additional information you offer can be visual or verbal in nature such as an on-site demonstration. Remember, if the *"I need more information"* objection comes before your presentation, your verbal presentation may suffice. If the *"I need more information"* objection comes after your presentation, it is a good indicator that you need something other than words — something tangible — and a printed, third-party endorsement such as an independent news or magazine article is best.

Reason to Buy. Many times you can make the customer's objection to your product or service the *reason to buy* and turn the perceived drawback of your product or service *into the selling benefit* that makes the sale.

If the customer says, *"Yours is too heavy!"*

You might respond by saying:

"Well Mr. Customer, that is correct. We have the heaviest unit on the market today and that is by design. Studies show the number one reason for mechanical failures is vibration. The lighter the unit, the more vibration. True, it might cost a little extra to

After the Sale **SALES SKILLS**

transport it, but wouldn't you rather have a unit that has a stellar reliability record and lasts years longer than one that is in the repair shop for mechanical repairs? Quite frankly, the added weight and quality that is built into our units is the top reason our customers purchase our unit over the competition's. Do you see how the additional weight actually makes for a better and more reliable product and works to your advantage?"

Remember, if the customer takes the time to ask a question or express an objection, you have the skills to handle it effectively and make it work for you rather than against you.

Your Mission

On the chart on the next page, list the 3-5 most common objections you have to handle concerning your product or service on the left side. To the right of the objection, write a statement that effectively handles the objection.

LICENSE TO SELL

Objection	How to Handle

After the Sale   **SALES SKILLS**

Negotiation Skills

The definition of negotiation is arriving at a settlement to deliver something in return for an equivalent value and to get through or around something successfully. One or all of these descriptors can be found in a sales negotiation. With competition fiercer than ever, many customers will not feel they have achieved the best purchase available unless some form of negotiation takes place.

Unfortunately, those unskilled in the art of negotiation often resort to reducing price as a means of satisfying the customer. And although splitting the difference between the price you are asking and the price the customer wants to pay is an acceptable negotiation technique, it is by far one of the worst when it comes to money.

A successful negotiation is one where everyone involved wins – or at a minimum feels that they are not being cheated or short-changed in the process.

When to Negotiate. We negotiate to get what we want. Ideally, no negotiation is necessary. In other words, you ask for something and you get it. However, when one party to a sale is unwilling to accept the terms and conditions that are on the table – to continue the process any further – odds are a negotiation must occur. The first pitfall many novice negotiators fall into is negotiating too soon in the process. Therefore, knowing when to negotiate is the first skill a professional negotiator learns. These four factors must exist for a negotiation to begin:

1) All parties have placed on the table all terms and conditions associated with the sale.

2) An issue or objection (could be multiple issues or objections) has been raised that cannot be overcome with benefits of the opposing negotiating party.

LICENSE TO SELL

3) No underlying objections or reasons are present aside from the issue or issues to be negotiated. In other words, if it were not for the issue or issues to be negotiated, a sale would be made.

4) There is conditional commitment; an implied agreement by all parties involved that if the negotiation is successful a sale between the parties will occur.

Starting with only two or three factors present will allow an escape hatch for one of the parties to exit, and thus shift the balance of power to one side. Even with these four factors on the table, it still does not prevent a party from walking away or negotiating in "bad faith." However, most of the time, customers you come in contact with will be sincere in their interest and willingness to negotiate.

The first two conditions actually occur during the sales process. Terms and conditions such as price and deliverables are discussed throughout the sale. Like any good salesperson, your job is to try and overcome all customer objections with the benefits of your product or service. Assuming the above two conditions have occurred and you are unable to support the customer's objection with benefits, only then are you ready to move to the third and fourth condition necessary for a negotiation to occur. Think of these conditions as the legs on a table. All four legs must be planted firmly on the ground before the weight of the negotiation is placed upon it. Otherwise, the table is bound to collapse as the negotiation proceeds.

The last two conditions are met with the asking of a few customer questions. How many questions you ask and the order in which you ask them will be a judgement call on your part. At a minimum, both conditions must be met. Ideally, not only are the conditions met once – but are twice confirmed.

Questions. The following questions are asked twice to confirm that conditions three and four have been met. The use of one or more of these questions may be necessary to judge if the conditions required for a negotiation to proceed have been met:

After the Sale **SALES SKILLS**

✔ *So aside from this one issue, you would purchase the product. Is that correct?*

✔ *Do you have any other objections, questions or issues before we address this issue?*

✔ *Is there anyone else who needs to be here to authorize the sale? So you have the complete authority to sign off on this deal, correct? You don't need to speak to (your wife, your boss, your accountant, your attorney, your religious leader, etc.)?*

✔ *There is nothing else preventing us from doing business today, aside from (state the issues), right?*

✔ *In essence, what you are saying is if we had to we could create an agreement with this one contingency that I would sign and that you would sign, correct?*

✔ *So, you are now ready to negotiate. Where do we start?*

Techniques & Strategies

Here are six techniques and various strategies to ensure you will be able to successfully negotiate yourself in, and out of, any situation you may encounter. The techniques are listed in the order in which they should be used. The techniques are:

✔ Benefits Alone

✔ Trade-Off

✔ Enhancement

✔ Split the Difference

✔ Concession

✔ Walk Away

Benefits Alone. This technique should always be employed first to ensure a negotiation is indeed necessary to resolve the issue. The very fact you are trying a second time to offset the customer's concerns and objections with existing or new benefits not previously mentioned, illustrates to the customer

LICENSE TO SELL

that you are sincere in your belief that the product or service is worth what you are asking for it. The tactic is also a defense against those customers who create an objection simply as a ploy to enter into a negotiation. They don't really have a goal other than to go through a round of negotiation to satisfy themselves that they just didn't accept the first sales offer. In this case, reassurance alone with existing or additional benefits is all that is necessary. Both the customer and the salesperson walk away with a win-win outcome.

Examples:

✔ Let's review exactly what you're getting for your money...

✔ When you consider all that you are getting, X, Y, and Z, isn't it worth the investment?

✔ Let me summarize what we've talked about up to now. I'm confident doing so will highlight the benefits associated with your decision to move forward.

✔ In addition to the benefits discussed, let me introduce to you a couple more I'm confident will more than outweigh your concerns.

✔ Here are a few more benefits that will easily tip the scales in your favor. They are...

Trade-Off. A trade-off is achieved when something is given in exchange for something else. If the customer wants a lower price, you give it to him, but at the same time reduce the deliverable – for example he takes the lower model. Trade-offs work in both directions. If the customer wants the better model, you give it to him, but charge him more for it. The use of the trade-off keeps the relative value of the price, terms and conditions. If the customer wants a little more or less in one area, you reduce or increase another area to maintain the relative balance of the deal. This technique has built into it a balance formula that helps ensure a win-win outcome.

After the Sale **SALES SKILLS**

Examples:

✔ *To allow the sale at the price you want, the service agreement must be reduced from three years to two.*

✔ *If we include the premium options you desire, the price will be 15% higher.*

✔ *To get at the price you want, I will need your participation in our customer marketing program. Specifically, it entails you providing me with the names and phone numbers of the 10 personal contacts you know who would have an interest in my product.*

Enhancement. This technique is one of the best negotiation techniques, yet is often the most overlooked. The last thing a salesperson typically wants to do is drop price. The main reason: You might be compensated based on a commission calculated off of the total sales price or evaluated based on monthly sales volume. Regardless, cutting price or deliverables should never be your second line of defense. An enhancement is just that – something you add to the deal to offset or satisfy the customer's objection. If it is price, add something to the deal that will be perceived as high-value to the customer but costs you and the company very little (e.g., an extended service agreement, free oil change, more training or personal support, etc.) Think back on qualifying statements the customer has made. When you prioritize their list, you will know what items are of high value to the customer. This approach allows you to make the sale and keep your price the same, giving up minimal concessions in exchange for gaining the customer agreement at full price.

Examples:

✔ *I can't reduce the price by $300, but to offset it, I can include technical support and training that has a $300 value.*

✔ *I am unable to deliver the product to you today. What if I was able to provide you today with a demo model and then replace it when the item comes in on Tuesday?*

LICENSE TO SELL

✔ *I am unable to bring the price any lower, but, what if I gave a complimentary room upgrade – that's a $50 value.*

✔ *The warranty is set by the factory, so extending it 1 year is beyond my control. What if I was able to offer a guaranteed trade-in allowance during the term of the contract instead?*

Split the Difference: Splitting the difference is one of the most common, often used negotiation techniques. The problem is that most novice negotiators go to this technique first and often end up giving away more than necessary to make the sale. Splitting the difference should be used on trivial or small negotiation issues as a means to gain agreement. It is used most often with price. You want $1,000 for the item, the customer is willing to pay $800 – so you split the difference and a sale is made at $900. When splitting the difference, it is not always a 50/50 split. It can be 60/40 or 70/30. The idea is that you end up somewhere between what the customer is offering and the price you stated.

You might see this as a negotiation – but as you can see, you gave up $100 to make the sale happen. What did you get in return aside from selling your product at a lower cost?

✔ Did you get the customer to give you the names of 10 people he knows (referrals) who might be interested in the product?

✔ Did you get the customer to agree to an extended service contract or to purchase replacement parts from you?

✔ Did you get the customer to agree to consider another product or service you have to offer at a future date?

Although an easy tactic to use, it should always be leveraged with something you want. Using some of the above strategies to get the customer to give you something in return for splitting the difference, turns the tactic into a trade-off. As you now know, a trade-off is a superior negotiation tactic because it maintains the balance of the price, terms and deliverables.

Examples:

✔ *You are offering me $800 and the price is $1,000. What if we were to call it a deal at $925?*

✔ *You want a 3-year warranty and the item only comes with a 6-month warranty. What if I brought it up to a full year?*

✔ *You want delivery tomorrow without having to pay an additional charge and our standard is 3-day delivery. What if I was able to bump it up to second-day air?*

Concession. A concession is your last resort. It is a negotiation tactic used when there are no other options left and you do want to earn the customer's business. A concession is when you give the customer what he wants and you get nothing in return. In theory, you should only offer concessions on small, trivial items. Unfortunately, it usually becomes an issue with price. With competition as fierce as it is, you would rather sell the item at cost than allow the customer to walk out the door.

Examples:

✔ *You drive a hard bargain, but it's a deal.*

✔ *If I get authorization to make this happen, we have an agreement. Correct?*

Walk-Away. A walk-away is your most powerful negotiation strategy. It is what keeps you and the other party at the table, because each knows at any time the other could decide to walk-away. When do you decide to walk-away? When the deal is no longer a win-win. Or, in other words, a lose for you. The walk-away is sometimes never used as an option. However, most complex or savvy negotiators will have no choice to define what their walk-away strategy is to the other party. Doing so defines the breaking point of the negotiation. It creates a temporary boundary the other party may use to ensure his suggested negotiation alternatives fall within.

Sometimes, the walk-away is not only threatened, but used as a tactic to make the sale. The customer walks-away and the salesperson allows him to walk out the door. This is done as a

LICENSE TO SELL

test to ensure the customer is indeed serious about that being his last and final offer. The salesperson then contacts the customer after he has left or while he is in the parking lot to continue the sale. Usually under some ploy, such as "my manager saw you leave and gave me permission to make the sale." Often the best price, terms and conditions are negotiated when both parties walk-away from the table at least once during the negotiation process. This is often the case in long or complex negotiations when talks end and resume again. Sometimes even a moderator or objective third party is necessary to keep the negotiation productive. If you walk-away, show regret, inform the other party why you are unable to continue and do your best to maintain the relationship.

Examples:

✔ *I appreciate your position. However, I am just unable to sell the product at that price. I appreciate your time but we just can't seem to reach agreement on this issue.*

✔ *You can't say we didn't try. Thank you for your time. If the price should change, I'll give you a call and let you know.*

✔ *The 3-year option is not something we have the ability to create. I wish it were. However, it appears to be your one deal-breaker of an issue and unfortunately I can't address it. If something should change in the future, I will let you know.*

Planning Your Negotiation Strategy

An important component of an effective negotiation strategy is one that is based on a plan. What follows are four steps you should use to create your plan.

1) Define and anticipate your offer and counteroffers.
2) Define and anticipate the customer's offer and counteroffers.
3) Identify and analyze your negotiation options.
4) Create, and stick to, a negotiation menu of acceptable option combinations.

Remember that the gap between your initial offer and your walk-away position is the room available for negotiation.

After the Sale — SALES SKILLS

Negotiation Tactics:

- ✔ Always place price, terms and conditions on the table before negotiating
- ✔ Add value to your offer or concession by making it look difficult
- ✔ Call a time-out if you need time to think, call someone, or review the offer that is on the table
- ✔ Flinch at the other party's first offer – psychologically, it puts you at an advantage
- ✔ Pause before responding to an offer
- ✔ Make your boss the bad guy
- ✔ Use "What if" so your offers remain hypothetical
- ✔ Listen actively, summarize and confirm understanding
- ✔ Put complex or important terms in writing
- ✔ Clarify vague statements
- ✔ Confirm and table all objections prior to all negotiating
- ✔ Be clear and concise in your offers
- ✔ Use trial balloons as a way to test your offers
- ✔ Don't be the first to name a price – if you must quote retail
- ✔ Temporarily put aside items with much disagreement
- ✔ Always couch your offers in terms of benefits to the other party
- ✔ Use positive body language
- ✔ Know, in advance, your walk-away position
- ✔ Never reveal your deadlines
- ✔ Be on the look out for sudden changes in body language
- ✔ Document and confirm all agreements
- ✔ Play dumb when you need time or additional information
- ✔ Counterbalance any buyer's remorse

LICENSE TO SELL

Common Negotiation Mistakes:

✔ Start negotiating too soon

✔ Wrong person or non-decision maker

✔ Just talking versus negotiating

✔ Win-lose mentality of either party

✔ No back-up plan or alternatives

✔ Take it or leave it ultimatums

✔ Allowing personalities to interfere with issues

✔ Using phases like, "Let me be honest with you..." and "trust me"

✔ Emotional outbursts

✔ Threats

✔ Omission of details that will be uncovered after the sale

✔ Minimal use of questions to clarify and confirm understanding

✔ Accepting the first offer made

✔ Being first/quick to name a price or to counter a price

✔ Not considering the impact of buyer's remorse

Where to Sit During a Negotiation:

✔ *1 on 1:* Sit facing the other person without barriers.

✔ *1 on 2:* Sit where you can see both people.

✔ *2 on 1:* Split up to provide two perspectives/voices.

✔ *Many on Some:* Stay together for power.

✔ *Some on Many:* Intermingle with group to diffuse their power.

After the Sale **SALES SKILLS**

When Negotiating Over the Phone:

✔ Be Prepared

✔ Confirm other party is prepared

✔ Minimize interruptions

✔ Use the hold or mute button as needed

✔ Call back if necessary

✔ Take notes

✔ Integrate your meeting with fax, e-mail, etc.

Properly Concluding the Negotiation:

✔ Express confidence in the other party and the overall agreement

✔ Review the agreement details to ensure no misunderstanding

✔ Confirm what the next steps in the process are – who does what

✔ Thank the other party for their time and consideration

You Know You've Negotiated Successfully When:

✔ Agreement reached is satisfactory to you, your company and your customer

✔ Both sides feel the other side was fair

✔ Both sides would do business with the other again

✔ Both sides can deliver (and do) what each promised

✔ When agreement is put in writing, both parties are willing and able to sign

LICENSE TO SELL

Your Mission

Review the six negotiation tactics (starting on page 185). Which tactics do you use currently?

_____
_____
_____
_____
_____

Which tactics do you want to use more?

_____
_____
_____
_____
_____

Which negotiation mistakes have you made in the past? What can you do to prevent them from happening again in the future?

_____
_____
_____
_____
_____

After the Sale							**SALES SKILLS**

Put Yourself Next in Line

Many salespeople work as much against themselves as for themselves. In essence, they tend to always measure their sales success as all or nothing. They either got the sale or they didn't. They know what to do when they get the sale, but it's when they don't get the sale that a big opportunity is lost. Most take the approach of thanking the customer for his time and then go off to the next customer as if the first customer never existed. Although this approach may be good in terms of clearing your mind of non-selling experiences and negative customer attitudes, it doesn't capitalize on the gains already made.

What gains? Well, if there were two companies vying for the same customer's business — yours and your competitor's, if the other salesperson wins the customer's business, where does that place you? Out in the cold? No. It places you in the runner-up position or second place.

Staying in the Race. Think of the process as a 3-year long race to get the customer's business. Your competition may be in first place now, but being in second place is the next best position. What happens if number one stumbles and falls? You are right there to take the lead. You can only do that if you are in the race. Think of selling as a marathon not a sprint. You can't win the marathon if you leave the race after the first mile or two.

Staying in the race means treating your big, profitable, or prestigious accounts as if they were already your customers. Simply call them every now and then. Stop by every now and then. Send them your newsletter. Invite them to your company events. Send tickets to a ball game. Bottom line: you let them know you want their business and are willing to earn it through demonstrated service and loyalty.

It's amazing how friendly salespeople are until you say no to what they are selling. Most smile, say thanks and leave never to be heard from again — they leave the race and go home. Some get mad, they insult you, belittle you, knock the competition, or ridicule your decision to choose the competitor. They too leave the race, but they burn every bridge before they leave.

LICENSE TO SELL

This leaves a negative impression with the customer who may be thinking *I'm glad I didn't do business with that guy* and even more significant, *I'll never call that guy or do business with his company ever!*

Like any race, odds are it is not going to be just you and another guy. It will probably be you and a handful of other competitors. However, only the real pros know how to run the race. Let's assume your proposal is one of many. If the other three competitors leave the race and go home, where does that put you? In second place! And just like a race, there is nothing to say that a moment before you are about to take the lead, a competitor jumps back in and cuts in front of you. It's more like a rat race with no rules. But more often than not, you will be greatly rewarded by your customers for staying in the race. It may take a month, a year, or even a decade, but the day you earn the business is the day you win the race.

Your Mission

Look through a database of past proposals where you did not get the contract. Select three and put a "second place" strategy together to win the customer's business. Who are the three customers?

1. _____

_____

2. _____

_____

3. _____

_____

After the Sale   **SALES SKILLS**

Follow-Up — You'll Be Hearing from Me

The number one way to differentiate yourself from your competitors and be a superior salesperson is to follow-up with your customers — on a consistent basis!

It really is that simple because, the vast majority of salespeople out there are order takers. They do not have good follow-up systems or procedures in place that would allow them to follow up. Too many salespeople do not put a high enough priority on follow-up.

Sales and marketing research over the years has supported these two theories:

- ✔ It takes nine impressions (contacts) to make an initial sale;
- ✔ It takes six impressions in a year (contacts) to maintain top-of mind awareness.

An impression can take many formats. It can be in the form of a letter, voice message, e-mail, brochure, contract proposal, advertisement, sending an article, or a personal call. Depending on your sales cycle, it can take up to nine different impressions to make the initial sale. Be consistent!

If you are number two in the customer's mind, it is even more important to stay in touch — so when number one stumbles, you are top of mind!

Keep in Touch. You should know by now that it costs less to do business with a satisfied customer than to constantly be prospecting for new ones. The point is once you have made a sale and built rapport, *keep in touch*! It is both smart business and could lead to referrals. Here are some suggestions on follow up approaches:

- ✔ A personalized thank you note after a sale is complete. A hand-written note is very effective.
- ✔ Send cards on birthdays, holidays, etc.

LICENSE TO SELL

- ✔ Clip articles from magazines/newspapers about your customer's business and send them to the customer. To make a lasting impression, have the article laminated with your business card at the bottom!
- ✔ Send out releases about your business which could include new products, renovations, or key personnel changes.
- ✔ Send postcards when you are on trips.
- ✔ Mail out regular company newsletters.
- ✔ Send regular e-mail messages, sometimes with just a joke or funny saying for the day.
- ✔ Send faxes announcing activities in the area such as an upcoming educational symposium at a local university.
- ✔ Make a personal call.
- ✔ Advertise and send copies of the ads to your customers.
- ✔ Create and maintain a fantastic web site.
- ✔ A fun idea is to start a "Cookie of the month club." Contract with a great bakery and have them ship a couple of dozen different cookies at the start of each month. Customers will be calling you with thanks. This idea works with other items like popcorn, chocolates, doughnuts, etc.

Friends of the Family. All customers are important, but some are a bit more important than others! For these, usually your top 20%, have a regular entertainment schedule that gets you and your top customers outside the office. This could include golf, fishing, theater, dinner in your home, or a day at the ballpark or speedway. When possible, include spouses — it helps attendance and builds goodwill.

Do you do this with every customer? Not likely — nor cost effective. At a minimum, you should be making six follow-up contacts a year with the top 20% of your customers. Chances are good they are producing 80% of your business! Do not take them for granted.

After the Sale **SALES SKILLS**

Your Mission

Form a picture in your mind of the top five customers or organizations you currently work with. These top five should be so significant that if you were to lose their business, it would be a blow and have to be replaced!

Next, make five copies of the following form entitled License to Sell Customer Profile. Complete as much of the personal information as you can on these top customers. There will be information you do not know. Finding out that missing information should be one of the objectives for your next appointment with that customer.

Customers are willing to give this to you if you have built a relationship on trust. Be prepared to share — the customer may want to know similar information about you!

Once you have the information, set up a reliable follow-up system that notes key dates for birthdays, entertainment opportunities, and holidays. Make this a priority. You do not want a competitor to know any of your customers better than you!

LICENSE TO SELL

License to Sell Customer Profile

CUSTOMER

Name:

Title:

How long in current job:

Previous jobs with this organization:

Other organizations worked for:

Administrative assistant's name:

EDUCATION

Where did they attend high school:

Where did they attend college:

Degrees earned:

Active in sorority / fraternity:

HOBBIES/INTERESTS

Active in particular sports:

Favorite sports team(s):

After the Sale   **SALES SKILLS**

Do they collect things: _____

Like to read books: _____

Memberships in Assn's/clubs: _____

Military service: _____

Political party preference: _____

LIFESTYLE

Vacation preferences: _____

Recent changes to note (health, moved, etc.): _____

Favorite drink: _____

Smoke (cigar, cigarettes): _____

Favorite restaurants/food type: _____

What kind of car: _____
Birthday: _____
Any knowledge of family: _____

What is current entertainment schedule with this customer: ___

LICENSE TO SELL

BUSINESS

Does current business volume rank this customer in your top 10:

If yes, what number:

What are the top needs of the customer:

Can you meet all those needs better than your competitors:

What is the number one advantage you hold over the competition:

Where are you most vulnerable to losing the business:

Additional notes:

SALES TIPS

TOP SECRET

If a competitor is able to get to your customer faster, better or less expensively than you can, a precedent has been set. It is only a matter of time before the customer will demand the same level of service from you.

TOP SECRET

The concept of real-time selling doesn't only apply to static information like rate sheets and brochures. Information in general — status reports, updates, current situations — can be real-time information.

TOP SECRET

Computers, interactive video-phones, the Internet, the telephone, and other technology will eliminate the reason for physically being on-site. Or, at least change the reason and frequency for physically being on-site.

TOP SECRET

The year 2000 and beyond sale will emphasize different selling features: consumer-based custom presentation; salesperson must be an expert.

TOP SECRET

Successful salespeople in the year 2000 and beyond are consultative.

TOP SECRET

Skilled 2000 and beyond salespeople will use strategic probing, along with strategic information gathering before interacting with customers.

TOP SECRET

Often, the sale is made when the customer realizes that it may cost more to do nothing about their current situation, than to do something about it.

TOP SECRET

Customers today and into the future expect straight answers to straight questions. Bottom line: there should be no doubt in the customer's mind that you possess expert product knowledge.

LICENSE TO SELL

TOP SECRET

The salesperson and company of the 21st century must be willing to change and adapt at a moment's notice.

TOP SECRET

A virtual company can change direction overnight by simply changing suppliers.

TOP SECRET

Partnering is a cost-effective alternative to carving out a customer base from an existing competitor market share. The best partners are those that offer complementary services, products or resources to one another.

TOP SECRET

If customers perceive they can get what they want, when they want it and know they can return it if it doesn't work — they will pay a little more for it if they can buy it from a company they can trust.

TOP SECRET

You must become your customer's ATM — regardless of the products or services you sell.

TOP SECRET

The new business attitude is to get it out the door first and fix any "bugs" in the next release.

TOP SECRET

Just as companies become virtual, so will salespeople who become more like symphony conductors or integrators. Their greatest skill will be their ability to meet the customers' needs by integrating all the vendors, suppliers and information sources together in the quickest period of time.

TOP SECRET

The emphasis of selling in the future will then be on comfort levels and overall trust of the company and the transaction process. Decisions will still be made based on facts — price, services, features, benefits, warranties, guarantees — but more than ever on perceptions rather than reality.

SALES TIPS

TOP SECRET

Smaller local vendors can compete against convenience, inventory and price by capitalizing on personalized service and expertise.

TOP SECRET

We hold a place in our marketing, sales and advertising brains for firsts, not seconds. Consequently, getting there first and staying there is a tremendous sales advantage.

TOP SECRET

You will increase your sales opportunities by keen listening to past and current customers. They have valuable knowledge to impart if you will listen and learn.

TOP SECRET

The way many companies will catch up with defect reduction is to outsource manufacturing, delivery and services to firms with better defect reduction methods.

TOP SECRET

Real-time access to knowledge, product information, competitor information, financing options, delivery schedules, etc., must be a click away.

TOP SECRET

It's in your best interest to complete the transaction as quickly and easily as possible.

LICENSE TO SELL

Notes: